Jeanne Casella and
Carolyn Barnett

ENGLISH

PLAIN AND

SIMPLE

AMSCO

When ordering this book, please specify:
either **R 260 W** or ENGLISH, PLAIN AND SIMPLE

AMSCO SCHOOL PUBLICATIONS, INC.
315 Hudson Street / New York, N.Y. 10013

ISBN 0-87720-396-2

Printed in the United States of America

Dear Teacher,

This textbook, aptly titled *English, Plain and Simple*, has three main objectives:

To teach those facts of grammar and usage paramount in common need and practice.

Included are the parts of speech; sentence structure; agreement; case; tense; punctuation; etc.

To teach fundamental, related skills of English.

Included are synonyms; homonyms; antonyms; vowel-consonant recognition; alphabetizing; dictionary use; avoidance of common errors; abbreviations; paragraph development; the friendly letter; handwriting; etc.

To make the all-important transition between language facts and their functional application in personal student expression.

Every experienced English teacher will at once recognize this objective as a cardinal need of English teaching.

The scope and methodology we have designed are specifically geared to a wide student audience in the following ways:

1. The scope is confined to what is practical and functional. All explicatory material—presentations, concepts, definitions—is kept *plain* and *simple*. Sentences are short. Words are understandable. Ideas are kept to their crispest form. Concrete examples are always included.

2. All exercises and assignments are realistic, written to offer reasonable learning challenges and to assure confidence-building degrees of success. Comprehensive reviews are included.

3. Exercises and assignments carefully build learning, step by step. First exercises are at the simple level of recognition drill. Concluding exercises call for personal, creative application.

4. The fun of successfully meeting mental challenges provides motivation. Liveliness has been augmented by other devices: simple diagramming, word games and language games, stimulating graphics, and opportunities for individual expression on meaningful topics.

We are confident that you and your students will use *English, Plain and Simple* with profit and pleasure.

The Publisher

chapter one NOUNS

chapter two PRONOUNS

chapter three VERBS

chapter four THE SIMPLE SENTENCE

chapter five ADJECTIVES

chapter six ADVERBS

chapter seven PREPOSITIONS

chapter one

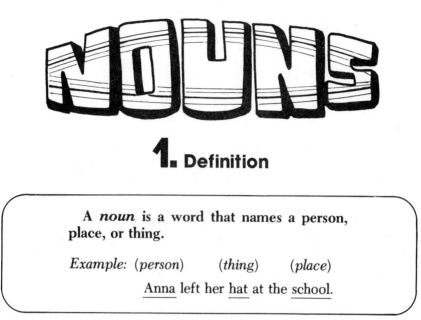

1. Definition

> A *noun* is a word that names a person, place, or thing.
>
> *Example:* (*person*)   (*thing*)   (*place*)
> Anna left her hat at the school.

The *noun* is the first of eight groups of words called the **parts of speech.** As we move forward in this book, we will study each of them. We will discover how they help us express ourselves clearly and interestingly.

A.   Underline the nouns in these sentences. The first sentence is done for you as an example.

1. Our school has a new gymnasium.

2. The cafeteria serves hot lunches.

3. This class is science.

4. Peter lost his watch on the bus.

5. Write a letter to Grandmother.

6. The earth is a planet.

7. Bill is the captain of the team.

8. The boy was polishing his motorcycle.

9. Men and women in the stands cheered the team.

10. In the office, Alice works on a computer.

B. Now that you have had practice with nouns, write some of your own.

PERSONS	PLACES	THINGS
_____	_____	_____
_____	_____	_____
_____	_____	_____
_____	_____	_____
_____	_____	_____
_____	_____	_____
_____	_____	_____

C. Write a noun that fits the sentence.

1. The _____ was given a medal.

2. A _____ repairs teeth.

3. The color of a ripe _____ is red.

4. Put a teaspoon of _____ in my tea.

5. The _____ keeps our school clean.

D. Write four sentences below. In each, use at least one of the nouns you wrote in Exercise B. First, turn back a page and look at the ten sentences. Notice that each starts with a capital (large) letter and ends with a period. Make sure that your sentences do, too.

1. _____

_____

2. _____

_____

3. _____

_____

4. _____

_____

English, Plain and Simple

Homonyms

Homonyms are two words that sound alike. Though they sound alike, they have different spellings and different meanings.

Examples: tail, tale
sight, site

A. Here are a dozen nouns. If you rearrange them properly on the lines below, you will have six pairs of homonyms. The two nouns in each pair will sound alike. Follow the model.

pail	mail	stake
sun	pale	flour
steak	son	knight
night	flower	male

1. <u>sun</u>   <u>son</u>

2. _____   _____

3. _____   _____

4. _____   _____

5. _____   _____

6. _____   _____

"Homonyms all sound alike to me!!"

B. After you are sure that your answers are correct for the exercise you have just done, fill in each blank in these sentences with the correct noun.

1. I like my _____ medium rare.

2. My brother got a package in the _____.

3. Who will fetch a _____ of water?

4. It takes two cups of _____ to make this cake.

5. The _____ swore to protect King Arthur.

6. Someone broke into their house during the _____.

7. The _____ is an important source of energy for heating homes.

8. The _____ on this plant will bloom all summer.

9. Josephine has recovered from the flu, but she still feels weak and looks _____.

10. Put another _____ in the ground to tie down the tent firmly.

2. Common and Proper Nouns

The word *boy* is a **common noun.** The name of a certain boy, *Jack Johnson,* is a **proper noun.** The difference between a common noun (C.N.) and a proper noun (P.N.) is made clear by the sentences below.

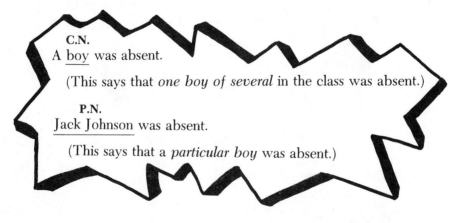

C.N.
A <u>boy</u> was absent.

(This says that *one boy of several* in the class was absent.)

P.N.
<u>Jack Johnson</u> was absent.

(This says that a *particular boy* was absent.)

Got the idea? Here are two more examples.

C.N.
The school has a new building.

P.N.
Redwood High School has a new building.

C.N.
We are reading a book this week.

P.N.
We are reading *Treasure Island* this week.

Common nouns are general names. *Proper nouns* are names of particular persons, places, or things.

Proper nouns should be capitalized.

Examples:

(*common nouns*)	(*proper nouns*)
boy ⟶	Jack
school ⟶	Redwood High School
book ⟶	*Treasure Island*

Two or more words, as you see, can be used together as a single proper noun. Which examples in the box show this? Notice that when a proper noun consists of more than one word, each important word begins with a capital letter.

A. Underline each noun. Put *C.N.* over the common nouns and *P.N.* over the proper nouns. The first sentence is a model.

C.N.   P.N.
1. Our school is located in the Central Valley.

2. The park we visited was Yellowstone in Wyoming.

3. Mrs. Mendes works as a cook in the cafeteria.

4. *Star Trek* is Janice's favorite show.

5. Mark rides a Honda to school.

B. Rewrite only the proper nouns in the list. Remember to capitalize them.

1. central park _____

2. river _____

3. city _____

4. park _____

5. mary _____

6. *gilligan's island* _____

7. movie _____

8. kings river _____

9. chicago _____

10. girl _____

C. Use proper nouns to answer the questions.

1. Who is your best friend? _____

2. What TV show do you like best? _____

3. What is your favorite song? _____

4. Where did you go to school last year? _____

5. In what state do you live? _____

D. Write common nouns in the blanks.

1. The _____ lost the game in the ninth inning.

2. In the summer we go to the _____ for swimming.

3. She's as quiet as a _____.

4. He wore a new _____ to school.

5. I like _____ better than any other food.

English, Plain and Simple

E. Write three sentences about things you have done this week. Then go back and underline the nouns.

1. _____

   _____

2. _____

   _____

3. _____

   _____

Time Out

You should be able to find at least 25 persons, places, or things in this puzzle. Some are common nouns; others are proper nouns. To help you get started, two words are circled.

A	P	E	Q	A	A	R	T	I	S	T	X	O
S	E	P	M	E	B	C	R	D	E	F	G	N
M	A	O	S	H	J	I	A	K	L	M	N	S
T	C	C	O	O	R	P	I	Q	R	S	T	E
N	H	W	N	I	A	T	N	U	O	M	U	R
L	A	T	G	V	T	W	X	Y	Z	A	A	E
B	L	X	H	I	G	F	E	G	D	N	C	B
R	I	C	K	A	R	B	O	X	C	D	E	D
O	Q	Z	O	D	M	L	V	U	W	X	Y	E
T	U	S	K	A	B	H	A	N	D	C	D	B
C	A	T	E	E	F	G	A	H	R	A	E	B
A	T	A	I	J	K	L	M	I	N	O	P	I
M	B	R	O	C	K	Q	E	U	R	O	P	E

Abbreviations

Sometimes you will want to abbreviate (shorten) proper nouns. Be sure you capitalize the abbreviation and put a period at the end.

Example: Thursday—<u>T</u>hurs<u>.</u>

Write these abbreviations correctly.

Days

sun _____

mon _____

tues _____

wed _____

thurs _____

fri _____

sat _____

States

ark _____
(Arkansas)

va _____
(Virginia)

ill _____
(Illinois)

mo _____
(Missouri)

calif _____
(California)

ky _____
(Kentucky)

If you don't know the abbreviations for other states, a dictionary will help you.

Months

jan _____

feb _____

mar _____

apr _____

(May, June, and July are not abbreviated.)

aug _____

sept _____

oct _____

nov _____

dec _____

Titles of Respect

dr _____
(Doctor)

mr _____
(Mister)

mrs _____
(Mistress)

sen _____
(Senator)

English, Plain and Simple

3. Compound Nouns

> A *compound noun* is made by joining two nouns together.
>
> *Examples:* steam + ship   = steamship
> pay   + roll   = payroll
> pot   + holder = potholder

The nouns in List A below joined to the nouns in List B will form compound nouns—if you match them correctly. *Hint:* start with the word in A and find the joining word in B. Write the whole word in the blank space. The first one has been done for you as an example.

List A	List B	
1. dish	shoe	dishwasher
2. straw	cake	_____
3. center	road	_____
4. wall	berry	_____
5. hour	case	_____
6. pan	ball	_____
7. foot	paper	_____
8. horse	glass	_____
9. rail	**washer**	_____
10. suit	piece	_____

Alphabetic Order

Often we must arrange words in alphabetic order, as the names of our classmates. At times, we must find words that have been listed alphabetically, such as (1) words in a dictionary; (2) names in a telephone book; (3) names and topics in an encyclopedia; and (4) authors, subjects, and book titles in a card catalog.

As you know, there are twenty-six letters in the alphabet. The letters *a, e, i, o,* and *u* are called **vowels.** All the rest are called **consonants.** How much do you remember about the order of these letters?

A. Can you enter the twenty-six letters of the alphabet in correct order? Write them across the lines. If you start each line with the letter indicated, then you know you are right.

A __ __ __ __ __ __ __ __ __

K __ __ __ __ __ __ __ __ __

U __ __ __ __ __

Which letters are vowels? __ __ __ __ __

What are the other letters called? _____

B. What letter comes before and what letter comes after each of these letters in our alphabet?

__ d __	__ k __	__ p __	__ s __
__ f __	__ g __	__ q __	__ w __
__ h __	__ r __	__ i __	__ j __
__ b __	__ e __	__ x __	__ n __
__ y __	__ v __	__ o __	__ c __
__ l __	__ t __	__ m __	__ u __

C. Put these nouns in the blank spaces in alphabetic order.

coach   1. _____

book   2. _____

pencil   3. _____

locker   4. _____

student   5. _____

handbook   6. _____

office   7. _____

football   8. _____

4. Plural of Nouns

A **singular noun** names one person (*boy*), place (*street*), or thing (*pen*).

A **plural noun** names more than one (*boys, streets, pens*).

A. Which are singular nouns? Which are plural? In the blank space, write *singular* or *plural* as the case may be.

1. rose _____

2. brushes _____

3. halves _____

4. story _____

5. lunch _____

6. firemen _____

Some plural nouns are formed by adding the letter **s** to the singular (animal—animals).

Some plural nouns add **es** to the singular (wish—wishes).

Some plurals make a change of letters (tooth—teeth).

What is the plural of *sky?* Do we add **s** or **es?** No. The correct spelling is *skies*. There are rules for forming plurals, and they are listed below.

> **(1) Most nouns form their plural by adding s.**
>
> table, tables; window, windows; school, schools

B. Write the plural of these words.

1. dog _____

2. pitcher _____

3. flower _____

4. bicycle _____

5. eagle _____

6. notebook _____

7. ocean _____

8. carpet _____

(2) **Nouns that end in s, ss, sh, ch, and x need an es for the plural ending.**

bus, buses; kiss, kisses; lash, lashes;
beach, beaches; wax, waxes

C. Write the plural of these words.

1. gas   _____

2. dish   _____

3. batch   _____

4. business   _____

5. bench   _____

6. box   _____

(3) **Many nouns ending in f or fe change f to v and add es.**

half, halves; life, lives

D. Write the plural of these words.

1. shelf   _____

2. leaf   _____

3. loaf   _____

4. knife   _____

5. thief   _____

6. wife   _____

(There are several exceptions to this guide, such as *chief—chiefs* and *roof—roofs*. You should check your dictionary if you are not sure of a plural form.)

(4) **If a noun ends in consonant + y, change the y to i and add es. If the noun ends in vowel + y, just add s.**

consonant + y: baby, babies; lady, ladies
    vowel + y: valley, valleys; monkey, monkeys

E. Write the plural of these words.

1. pony   _____

2. tray   _____

3. turkey   _____

4. sky   _____

5. joy   _____

6. party   _____

> **(5) There are some nouns that change their spelling completely to form the plural.** (Check the dictionary if you are in doubt.)
>
> man, men; child, children

F. Write the plural of these words.

1. woman   _____

2. tooth   _____

3. goose   _____

4. policeman   _____

5. foot   _____

6. louse   _____

G. Write the plural of each noun.

1. a spoon   some s<u>poons</u>

2. a bush   two b_____

3. that thief   these t_____

4. the policeman   several p_____

5. this peach   many p_____

6. one berry   these b_____

7. a calf   twin c_____

8. one goose   three g_____

9. this leaf   those l_____

10. a towel   several t_____

11. a woman   two w_____

12. the monkey   many m_____

13. my wife   their w_____

14. a wish   some w_____

15. that turkey   those t_____

5. Possessive Nouns

> A *possessive noun* shows ownership, or possession.

There are three simple rules for forming possessives.

(1) A singular noun forms the possessive by adding an apostrophe (') and an <u>s</u>.

girl, girl's; James, James's

(2) A plural noun ending in <u>s</u> forms the possessive by just adding an apostrophe.

boys, boys'; friends, friends'

(3) A plural noun that does not end in s forms the possessive by adding an apostrophe and an s.

men, men's; children, children's

A. Write the possessive noun in each of the following. Before you decide whether to add an apostrophe alone or an apostrophe plus *s*, ask yourself this question. Is the italicized word singular or plural?

1. She went to the office of the *principal.*

   She went to the _____ office.

2. The roadrunner, a bird, is the mascot of our *school.*

   The roadrunner is our _____ mascot.

3. On top of the mountain, we saw the nest of an *eagle.*

   On top of the mountain, we saw an _____ nest.

4. The make-up of the *actors* was heavy.

   The _____ make-up was heavy.

5. The downpour soaked the coats of the *children.*

   The downpour soaked the _____ coats.

6. The jacket belonging to *Mr. Jones* is yellow.

   _____ jacket is yellow.

7. The lines of the *actress* were hard to learn.

   The _____ lines were hard to learn.

8. The track record of *Bess* is great.

   _____ track record is great.

9. The voices of the *students* fell to a whisper.

   The _____ voices fell to a whisper.

10. The speeches of the *women* began the program.

    The _____ speeches began the program.

B. Place the apostrophe in the correct place in each of the following possessive nouns. You will have to decide by the meaning of the sentence whether it is a plural or a singular possessive.

1. The judges robe is black.
2. Two soldiers uniforms are hanging in the prop room.
3. Joes photograph is on the wall.
4. Mary borrowed Franks records.
5. Tourists enjoy Californias climate.
6. The tables leg was broken.
7. The trouts weight was three pounds.
8. Several womens coats were lying on the bed.
9. I sat down calmly in the dentists chair.
10. Don't go too close to the fans blade.

C. Some well-known phrases contain possessive nouns. Fill the blanks with the matching possessives selected from the list. The first one is done for you.

writer's	1. ___Lord's___	Prayer
snail's	2. _____	broomstick
witch's	3. _____	foot
Lord's	4. _____	greetings
catcher's	5. _____	pace
lovers'	6. _____	pet
teacher's	7. _____	cramp
season's	8. _____	quarrel
athlete's	9. _____	eye
bull's-	10. _____	apple
Adam's	11. _____	mitt

English, Plain and Simple

WRITE ON !

$\overline{A}$ $\overleftarrow{a}$ _____

_____

$\overleftarrow{B}$ $\overrightarrow{b}$ _____

_____

C $č$ _____

_____

Anne _____

_____

Bob _____

_____

Carol _____

_____

ape _____

_____

boy _____

_____

cake _____

_____

6. Review

A. What is a noun? _____

_____

B. Underline the nouns in these sentences.

1. Jim mows lawns after school and on Saturdays.

2. Wasps built nests under the roof of our garage.

3. Wolves will hunt at any time of day or night.

4. The men and women wrapped the packages of meat for the freezer.

5. The storm began in the Atlantic Ocean off the coast of Florida.

C. In some of these sentences, one word has been incorrectly used in place of its homonym. First, cross out the incorrect word. Then write the homonym that correctly fits the meaning of the sentence. If the sentence is correct, just write *C*.

1. The rose is a beautiful flour. _____

2. Tell the post office to hold your male while you are away. _____

3. I ordered my stake well done, not rare. _____

4. A knight in the Middle Ages wore armor into battle. _____

5. This park near the lake is a good sight for a picnic. _____

6. Pie crust is made with flour, water, and shortening. _____

7. The builder drove a steak into the ground to mark the boundary line. _____

8. Is your daughter older or younger than your sun? _____

9. There will be a sale on winter coats after the holidays. _____

10. If that TV movie is another horror tail, I do not want to watch it. _____

English, Plain and Simple

D. Change the common noun to a proper noun. Rewrite each sentence completely. The first sentence is rewritten as a model.

1. **I will meet you one day.**
   I will meet you on Saturday.

2. Will you go to the *movies* with me?

3. Let's go to the *park*.

4. Please buy the *magazine* for me.

5. One *student* was absent today.

6. How did you spend the *holiday*?

7. I called a *girl* yesterday.

8. How far are we from the *city*?

9. You will enjoy reading a *book*.

10. You can always count on help from a *friend*.

E. Make a compound noun by choosing a word from the box to add to the word on the left. The word you form must match the definition in parentheses.

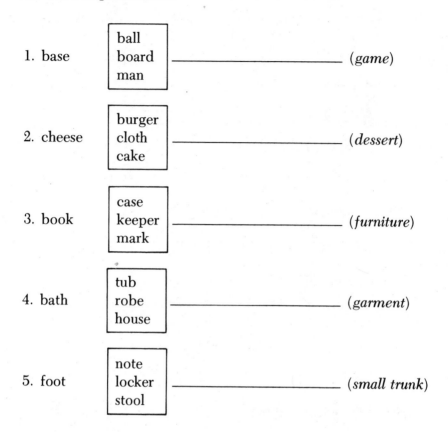

1. base   ball / board / man   _____ (*game*)

2. cheese   burger / cloth / cake   _____ (*dessert*)

3. book   case / keeper / mark   _____ (*furniture*)

4. bath   tub / robe / house   _____ (*garment*)

5. foot   note / locker / stool   _____ (*small trunk*)

F. Write the following nouns.

1. the singular of *feet*   _____

2. the plural of *car*   _____

3. the plural of *box*   _____

4. the singular of *donkeys*   _____

5. the singular of *candies*   _____

6. the plural of *lunch*   _____

7. the singular of *teeth*   _____

8. the singular of *knives*   _____

9. the plural of *story*   _____

10. the plural of *woman*   _____

English, Plain and Simple

G. Write the possessive noun in each of the following.

1. The population of Canada is smaller than that of Mexico.

   _____ population is smaller than Mexico's.

2. We were discussing the speech of the president.

   We were discussing the _____ speech.

3. The jacket of the skier is warm and light.

   The _____ jacket is warm and light.

4. All coats for men are on sale.

   All _____ coats are on sale.

Time Out

These nouns can have their letters rearranged to spell another noun. Can you do this? Be sure the words you write are nouns!

pot   _____

spot   _____

pit   _____

spear   _____

diet   _____

team   _____

hose   _____

art   _____

lime   _____

gates   _____

chapter two

1. Definition

A *pronoun* is a word that takes the place of a noun.

A pronoun is a small but important word. It keeps us from repeating a noun.

PARAGRAPH 1

This paragraph mentions *Jodi* and *Jodi's brother* so often that the paragraph sounds funny.

> Jodi was reading the newspaper want ads. Jodi wanted to find an after school job. Jodi planned to earn some extra money so Jodi could buy Jodi's brother the new tape player Jodi's brother wanted for Jodi's brother's car. Jodi wanted to earn money as soon as Jodi could because tape players are expensive. The tape player would be a special birthday surprise for Jodi's brother.

In paragraph 1, *Jodi* is used six times, and *Jodi's brother* four times.

PARAGRAPH 2

This paragraph uses pronouns in place of *Jodi* and *Jodi's brother*. The paragraph is smoother and more interesting, isn't it?

> Jodi was reading the newspaper want ads. She wanted to find an after school job. She planned to earn some extra money so she could buy her brother the new tape player he wanted for his car. Jodi wanted to earn money as soon as she could because tape players are expensive. The tape player would be a special birthday surprise for him.

In paragraph 2, *Jodi* appears only twice, and *Jodi's brother* not at all. *Jodi* is replaced with the pronouns *she* and *her*. *Jodi's brother* is replaced with the pronouns *he*, *his*, and *him*.

Do you now see how pronouns help us to speak better and write better?

2. Personal Pronouns

> **A *personal pronoun* can take the place of a "person" noun.** We can say
>
> *Alice* was reading the newspaper.
> or: *She* was reading the newspaper.
>
> **All personal pronouns can refer to persons, except *it*.** The pronoun *it* stands for a "place" noun or a "thing" noun. We can say
>
> A *tape player* is expensive.
> or: *It* is expensive.

A. Below is a list of personal pronouns. Study them carefully. Then cover the list and try to write the pronouns from memory.

I—me   _____   _____

he—him   _____   _____

she—her   _____   _____

we—us   _____   _____

they—them   _____   _____

you   _____

it   _____

B. Which words will complete these blanks?

He is to *him* as *she* is to _____, and as *I* is to _____.

We is to *us* as *they* is to _____.

It is to *it* as *you* is to _____.

C. In each sentence, write a pronoun that will take the place of the words in parentheses. Study the model sentences.

1. (*The visitors*) ___They___ did not stay long.

2. (*Yourself*) ___I___ study hard.

3. (*Your friends and yourself*) ___We___ went to the movies.

English, Plain and Simple

4. (*Eisenhower*) _____ was a president.

5. The teacher gave (*Joan*) _____ an "A."

6. Mary lost (*the book*) _____.

7. I will help (*a person to whom you are talking*) _____.

8. They went to the movies with (*your family and yourself*) _____.

9. We want to play football with (*the boys down the street*) _____.

10. I found (*the shoe*) _____ under the couch.

3. Possessive Pronouns

A word that shows ownership is a *possessive*. A noun can show ownership. We studied *possessive nouns* on page 14.

1. This is *John's* coat.

   (This sentence means: The coat belongs to John.)

A pronoun can also show ownership.

2. This is *my* coat.
3. This coat is *mine*.

   (*My* and *mine* are **possessive pronouns.**)

As in sentence 1 above, we add an *apostrophe* to a noun to form a possessive noun. On the other hand, **we do not use an apostrophe in a possessive pronoun.** In sentence 3, for example, we would NOT SAY, "This coat is mine's."

A. At the left is a list of the possessive pronouns. Write them in the proper blanks.

my, mine   1. That is _____ book.

That book is _____ .

his   2. _____ hat was lost.

The hat was _____ .

her, hers   3. _____ car was in the garage.

The car in the garage was _____ .

our, ours   4. It was _____ car that was wrecked.

The wrecked car was _____ .

their, theirs   5. We ran on _____ track.

The track we ran on was _____ .

your, yours   6. Take _____ dirty clothes to the cleaners.

These dirty clothes are _____ .

its   7. The dog ate _____ dinner.

B. Replace the underlined words with a possessive pronoun. Write the complete sentence on the blank line.

1. **John lost a pencil that belonged to him.**
   John lost his pencil. _____

2. Mr. and Mrs. Mason's house burned down.

   _____

3. The cat owned by Janet won a blue ribbon.

   _____

4. My family's friends are coming to visit us.

   _____

26   *English, Plain and Simple*

5. The leaves <u>on the tree</u> turn yellow in the fall.

---

4. Who, Which, and That

Another kind of pronoun is the **relative pronoun.** *Who, which,* and *that* are relative pronouns.

Who refers to persons only.

> The girl *who* fell sprained her ankle.

That refers to persons or things.

> I know the man *that* (or *who*) bought this store.
> A ball *that* clears the fence is a home run.

Which refers to animals or things, never to persons.

> The dogs *which* (or *that*) were trained by the police now guard the stations.

NEVER: A man *which* (use *who* or *that*) called left a message for you.

A. Fill in the blanks with the correct relative pronouns.

1. John is the one _____ caught the pass.

2. The clothes _____ I wear for gym are green.

3. The country _____ produces a lot of sugar is Cuba.

4. Are you the one _____ caught the biggest fish?

5. I like food _____ smells good and tastes delicious.

B. In each sentence, cross out the incorrect relative pronoun and write the correct one above. If it is correct, write a *C* above it.

1. The man which lives down the street is a doctor.

2. I like a dog who does tricks.

3. The bus that he took was late.

4. The magazine who sells more copies than any other is *Time*.

5. Is she the student which won the award?

6. Is that the camera who you got for your birthday?

7. The teenagers who belong to the rock group are seniors.

8. She has a dog which can be trained easily.

9. Drivers that do not use seat belts take a great risk.

10. These are the kittens who are for sale.

Time Out

The words below rhyme with one or more of the pronouns we have studied. Rhyming with *pie*, as an example, are the pronouns *I* and *my*. So they were written in the blanks. Now you do the rest.

pie	*I*	*my*	fur	___
pear	___		quiz	___
chore	___		new	___
tree	___	___	pat	___
	___	___	pitch	___
trim	___		sour	___
fit	___		say	___
nine	___		fuss	___

English, Plain and Simple

WRITE ON!

D d _____

E e _____

_____

F f _____

_____

Dave _____

_____

Earl _____

_____

Fred _____

_____

day _____

_____

every _____

_____

fun _____

_____

5. Review

A. Write the meaning of the word *pronoun*. _____

_____

B. Replace the underlined words by writing the *personal pronouns* above them.

1. The parents were playing cards.

2. Greg will start the game.

3. Mrs. Miller gave the award to Toni.

4. Can you name the Great Lakes?

5. Miss Jackson is the new teacher.

C. Replace the underlined words by writing the *possessive pronouns* above them.

1. Did Ida fix Ida's bike?

2. Did the cat eat the cat's food?

3. That is José's sweater.

4. My family will go in my family's car.

5. Those teachers really care about the teachers' students.

D. Fill in each blank with the correct possessive pronoun.

(my, mine)	1. There is _____ brother.
(her, hers)	2. I think that coat is _____ .
(our, ours)	3. It was _____ mistake.
(their, theirs)	4. The last house on the street is _____ .
(your, yours)	5. Is this shopping cart _____?

English, Plain and Simple

E. Complete the second sentence in each pair by writing pronouns. The pronouns you use should take the place of persons or things that are mentioned in the first sentence.

1. Ted and Mick avoid eating in the school cafeteria. On sunny days, you will find _____ eating _____ lunch in the park.

2. Since the bus strike, Bert has been driving Mrs. Diaz to the supermarket twice a week. _____ helps _____ because _____ has no car.

3. Nothing can come between Millie and her camera. In fact, _____ never leaves home without _____.

4. While your father and I are out shopping, please take down any telephone messages. Write _____ on this pad and tell whoever calls that _____ will return in about an hour.

F. Fill in each blank with the correct relative pronoun.

1. An evergreen is a plant _____ stays green all year.
2. George will decide _____ will get the award for the best speech.
3. They ate at a restaurant _____ overlooks the Pacific Ocean.
4. We are the ones _____ thought of the idea.
5. The air _____ we breathe is mostly oxygen.

G. Complete these sentences in a sensible way.

1. The teacher *who* _____

_____

2. Buy a sweater *that* _____

_____

3. A food *which* _____

_____

4. Tell your friends *that* _____

_____

5. A holiday *which* _____

_____

H. Rewrite this short paragraph, using pronouns where you think they are needed.

Mrs. Fiore, the principal, told Brooke that Brooke was being tardy too often. The principal asked Brooke what Brooke could do about the problem of being tardy. Brooke told the principal that Brooke would get up earlier and that lateness would not happen again.

_____

_____

_____

_____

_____

_____

_____

_____

_____

chapter three

1. Action Verbs

> An *action verb* shows action.
>
> My dog *barks* at strangers.
> I *studied* until midnight.
>
> Action verbs express not only *physical* action (like *barks* above), but also *mental* action (like *studied* above).

A. Fill in the blank with an action verb.

1. Elaine's father _____ houses.

2. Her mother _____ her own business.

3. Switzerland _____ cheese.

4. Horace _____ lunch at McDonald's.

5. Judy _____ when someone tickles her.

B. Underline the verbs in these paragraphs.

1. Jesse likes bowling. He bowls every Saturday. Last year he bought his own shoes and ball. Jesse holds the record for "high series" in the Junior League. He went to the state tournament. He brought home a second-place trophy.

2. Jesse's father works on his car all the time. Sometimes Jesse helps him. Yesterday they changed the spark plugs. They also cleaned the carburetor. Jesse's father takes good care of his car.

C. Alphabetize these verbs. Since they all begin with the same first letter, you will have to look at the second and sometimes even the third letter for alphabetizing.

believe   1. _____

build   2. _____

begin   3. _____

buy   4. _____

boil   5. _____

blame   6. _____

bake   7. _____

behave   8. _____

bite   9. _____

blow   10. _____

D. Some words can be used as nouns or verbs. Write *N* if the italicized word is a noun. Write *V* if it is a verb. (Remember, nouns name persons, places, or things. Action verbs show action.)

_____ 1. José *marches* in our school band.

_____ 2. John Philip Sousa wrote many *marches*.

_____ 3. The men in the safari went on a lion *hunt*.

_____ 4. Please *hunt* for the missing jigsaw piece.

_____ 5. She put some medicine on her mosquito *bites*.

_____ 6. The cat *bites* when people bother it.

_____ 7. They *paint* houses for extra money.

_____ 8. Put the *paint* in the jar.

_____ 9. *Post* the notice on the bulletin board.

_____ 10. He tied his horse to the *post*.

_____ 11. *Rose* plays tennis well.

_____ 12. In the garden, I picked a *rose*.

_____ 13. Joe Louis *rose* from poor farmboy to champion boxer.

_____ 14. We need two large *bowls* for the potato salad.

_____ 15. Sharon *bowls* on Saturday afternoon.

Antonyms

An *antonym* is a word that means the
opposite of another word.

love—hate
open—close

Replace the underlined action verb with a word that gives the
sentence an opposite meaning. Write the word (antonym) in the
blank space. The first sentence is done for you as a model.

__bought_____ 1. Jim <u>sold</u> his friend's TV set.

_____ 2. Jane <u>remembered</u> the answer to
that question.

_____ 3. If she <u>misses</u> the free throw, she
gets one point.

_____ 4. Almost everyone <u>loves</u> spinach.

_____ 5. Luke stepped on the brake and
<u>started</u> the car.

_____ 6. The rabbit <u>disappeared</u> in the ma-
gician's hat.

_____ 7. He <u>asked</u> the question correctly.

_____ 8. The police <u>released</u> the robber.

_____ 9. Please <u>close</u> the door so the breeze
will cool the house.

_____ 10. If you <u>play</u> hard, you will be paid
well.

English, Plain and Simple

2. Verbs of "Being"

> **The verb *to be* is a strange one. It changes form in sentences.**
>
> Ida wants TO BE a dancer.
> I AM a dancer.
> She IS a dancer.
> Leonard WAS a dancer.
> Ida and Leonard ARE dancers.
> They WERE dancers.

A. Circle the correct answers in the two sentences that follow each example sentence.

1. I *am* not old enough to drive yet.

   This sentence is speaking of (one, more than one) person.

   This sentence is speaking of (present, past) time.

2. Juan *is* a friend.

   This sentence is speaking of (one, more than one) person.

   This sentence is speaking of (present, past) time.

3. Jim Brown *was* captain of the football team.

   This sentence is speaking of (one, more than one) person.

   This sentence is speaking of (present, past) time.

4. They *are* in the school play.

   This sentence is speaking of (one, more than one) person.

   This sentence is speaking of (present, past) time.

5. His friends *were* late for the party.

   This sentence is speaking of (one, more than one) person.

   This sentence is speaking of (present, past) time.

B. Write the answers to the following questions.

1. Which italicized verbs in the previous exercise show present time?

   _____

2. Which italicized verbs show past time?

   _____

3. Which verbs were used with just one person?

   _____

4. Which verbs were used with more than one person?

   _____

C. Complete each sentence with the correct verb of being: *am, is, are, was,* or *were.*

1. I _____ on the phone. Please wait until I finish talking.

2. My parents _____ with the principal. They will finish their meeting soon.

3. A visitor _____ at school yesterday.

4. At this moment, she _____ outside in the yard.

5. France and England _____ on our side in World War II.

3. Helping Verbs

You have learned that the verb of a sentence shows action or "being."

ACTION: Ed *ran* to catch the bus.
BEING: Edna *was* not in school today.

Now read the following sentence:

Hilda was learning to play the guitar.

In the above sentence, we find two words that are verbs. *Learning* is an action verb, and *was* is a form of the verb *be*. Together, they form the complete verb *was learning*.

Learning is called the **main verb,** and *was* is called a **helping verb.**

The verb *be*, then, can be used as a main verb to show being (Lena *is* my neighbor) or as a helper to a main verb (Joe *is* moving south).

Most helping verbs fall into these groups.

BE	HAVE	DO	CAN	MAY	WILL	SHALL
am	has	does	could	might	would	should
is	had	did		must		
are						
was						
were						
been						
being						

A. Underline the complete verb in each of these sentences.

1. He was writing a letter to a friend.
2. They do make delicious pies.
3. Americans are using less energy now.
4. Jack will help with the decorations.
5. I should go to the dentist.
6. They must be in the backyard.
7. She does try her hardest.
8. Annette is drying her hair.
9. The plumber has repaired the leak in the kitchen.
10. They can water-ski in the bay.

English, Plain and Simple

(Sometimes there is more than one helping verb before the main verb in a sentence. See if you can underline all the verbs in these sentences.)

11. Ann should have arrived by now.
12. I must have given you the wrong address.
13. She may have taken the wrong turnoff.
14. I have been working in the cafeteria this week.
15. He should be elected president.

B. Look again at the complete verbs you underlined in Exercise A. For each one, write the main verb and the helping verb (or verbs) in the correct columns below. The first one has been done for you.

HELPING VERB (OR VERBS)	MAIN VERB
1. was	writing
2.	
3.	
4.	
5.	
6.	
7.	
8.	
9.	
10.	
11.	
12.	
13.	
14.	
15.	

C. Answer the following questions in complete sentences. Use some helping verbs.

1. What are you going to do after school today?

   _____

   _____

2. Where would you like to go on your vacation?

   _____

   _____

3. Have you read today's newspaper?

   _____

   _____

Thirteen verbs will complete this crossword puzzle. Study the clues ACROSS and DOWN. Then fill in the open spaces with the correct verbs.

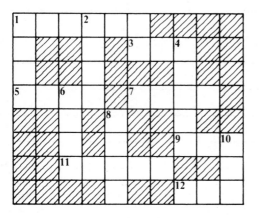

ACROSS

1. They will _____ for the lost boy.

3. _____ your vegetables.

5. I _____ ice cream.

7. He can _____ the piano.

9. _____ a home run.

11. Did you _____ at the joke?

12. Did he _____ the money he owed you?

DOWN

1. They will _____ their house, since they are moving.

2. He _____ on the palomino horse.

4. _____ me how to ski.

6. Poison will _____ you.

8. _____ the door.

10. If at first you don't succeed, _____ again.

4. Main Verbs and the Helping Verbs Have, Has, Had

As you realize, certain verbs change form according to how they are used. For example, *go* can change to *went* and *gone*. With the helping verbs *have*, *has*, and *had*, we must use *gone*, not *went*. In sentences:

WE CANNOT SAY	WE MUST SAY
I *have went* to bed.	I *have gone* to bed.
He *has went* to bed.	He *has gone* to bed.
She *had went* to bed.	She *had gone* to bed.

COLUMN 1	COLUMN 2
NEVER use the helpers *have*, *has*, and *had* with these verbs.	**ALWAYS** use the helpers *have*, *has*, and *had* with these verbs.
went	gone
did	done
wrote	written
drew	drawn
came	come
ate	eaten
rode	ridden
sang	sung
saw	seen
took	taken

A. Complete these sentences with verbs from Column 1. Make sure that, in each sentence, the verb you choose fits the sense of the sentence.

1. He _____ his name on the chalkboard.

2. Pat _____ the lucky number.

3. They _____ from another state.

4. The girl _____ old-fashioned songs with the band.

5. Kim _____ a shower.

B. Complete these sentences with verbs from Column 2. Choose verbs that make sensible sentences.

1. Jenny has _____ her homework.

2. Have you ever _____ frog legs?

3. Pete has _____ on a plane many times.

4. You should have _____ his face.

5. Paula has _____ her picture for the yearbook.

C. Insert a verb in each sentence below. If there is a helper in the sentence, choose a verb from Column 2. If there is no helper, choose a verb from Column 1. Be sure that your sentences make sense. The first two sentences are done for you.

1. He __went__ home after school.

2. Kathy had __seen__ the movie twice.

3. I have _____ my friends an invitation to my party.

4. He _____ a horse in the parade.

5. I _____ dinner early.

6. Jones has _____ to football practice, but he will be back soon.

7. Have you _____ your new bicycle yet?

8. Carla _____ her best on the test.

9. After they had _____ two songs, they left.

10. The artist has _____ a picture of me.

Time Out

Someone was sloppy when making these signs. All are misspelled. Can you straighten them out?

Contractions

In conversation, we often hurriedly say "I'm ready," or "It's raining." Such words as *I'm* and *it's* are called *contractions*. In these examples, *I am* is shortened to *I'm*, and *it is* to *it's*.

> A *contraction* joins two words and leaves out a letter or two. An *apostrophe* takes the place of the missing letter or letters.
>
> **he'll** = he will
> **they're** = they are

A. Underline the contraction in each sentence and write the two words from which it is made.

1. We've eaten already. _____ _____

2. I'll be glad to come. _____ _____

3. You're late. _____ _____

4. She's a very nice person. _____ _____

5. I'm sorry I was away. _____ _____

6. I've enough money for the movie. _____ _____

7. He's my partner. _____ _____

8. We're leaving soon. _____ _____

9. They've broken the computer. _____ _____

10. You've been fair. _____ _____

11. She'll run in the race. _____ _____

12. It's getting late. _____ _____

13. He'll follow us. _____ _____

14. They're coming into view. _____ _____

15. You'll need to be careful. _____ _____

B. Write the contraction made by joining the two words in parentheses.

1. (*They are*) _____ late again.

2. (*She will*) _____ go bowling with us.

3. (*I am*) _____ going to write to him.

4. (*I have*) _____ a dime if you need one.

5. Do you think (*he will*) _____ play tennis today?

6. (*It is*) _____ only a short distance from Washington, D.C., to Virginia.

7. (*You are*) _____ driving a new car.

8. I know that (*we are*) _____ always welcome.

9. (*We have*) _____ answered that question.

10. (*You will*) _____ hear from me soon.

WRITE ON!

$\mathcal{G}$ g _____

_____

$\mathcal{H}$ h _____

_____

$\mathcal{I}$ i _____

_____

Gary _____

_____

Harry _____

_____

Ivan _____

_____

goggles _____

_____

huge _____

_____

it _____

_____

5. Review

A. What is a verb? _____

_____

B. Underline the verbs in these sentences.

1. Paul lives in the Midwest.

2. He is in the store.

3. Inez took these pictures.

4. I was helping my little sister.

5. We visited a newspaper office.

6. You may go to the park.

7. Tom Sawyer had many exciting adventures.

8. Lee has written many good stories.

9. They are nice people.

10. This cake tastes very good.

C. Classify the underlined word as noun (*N*) or verb (*V*).

_____ 1. Jodi studies very hard.

_____ 2. She finished her studies.

_____ 3. She can play the piano.

_____ 4. The play was performed by the class.

_____ 5. He will polish his mother's furniture.

_____ 6. Jacob used the polish on his motorcycle.

_____ 7. Eva's bowling score-sheet shows three strikes in a row.

English, Plain and Simple

_____ 8. A careful person never <u>strikes</u> a match near a gasoline pump.

_____ 9. You <u>change</u> your hairstyle every month.

_____ 10. I have some <u>change</u> in my coat pocket.

D. Match each numbered word with its antonym at the right. Write the letter of the antonym in the space provided.

_____ 1. tell   *a.* cry

_____ 2. buy   *b.* stop

_____ 3. laugh   *c.* tighten

_____ 4. start   *d.* take

_____ 5. loosen   *e.* forget

_____ 6. shout   *f.* sell

_____ 7. remember   *g.* ask

_____ 8. close   *h.* harden

_____ 9. give   *i.* open

_____ 10. soften   *j.* whisper

E. Write the correct verb form for each sentence.

1. (**saw, seen**)   Christina _____ a UFO.

                     Amy has _____ the Daytona 500.

                     Have you _____ Louise today?

2. (**did, done**)   We _____ our homework quickly.

                     We have _____ our best.

                     Mr. Salas gave Luis a job, and he _____ it well.

3. (**went, gone**)   Carey _____ to the office.

                     No one has _____ home yet.

                     The principal had _____ home.

4. (**came, come**)   Juan had _____ from Mexico.

José _____ later.

Will Marie _____, too?

5. (**drew, drawn**)   She _____ a sketch of her friend.

She had not _____ it well.

What number has he _____?

F.   Combine each pair of words into a contraction. Write a sentence for each contraction.

1. (**It is**)   _____   _____

_____

2. (**They are**)   _____   _____

_____

3. (**I am**)   _____   _____

_____

4. (**You have**)   _____   _____

_____

5. (**She will**)   _____   _____

_____

Time Out

Fill the blanks with letters that spell a small word inside a larger word. Follow the model.

1. LA_N_I_ERN   Put "a small insect" inside "something that gives light to see by."

2. B__ __ __AR   Put "what a chicken lays" inside "someone who begs."

3. S__ __ __L   Put "something that you drink" inside "a word that means to rob."

4. ST__ __ __ __S   Put "something that you breathe" inside "something that you climb."

5. S__ __ __PER   Put "a part of your face" inside "a thing you wear on your foot."

chapter four

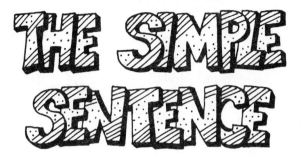

1. The Subject and Verb of a Sentence

> A sentence contains a *subject* and a *verb*.
>
> $\quad$ S $\quad\quad$ V
> The goldfish died.
>
> S $\quad$ V
> She is my English teacher.

Notice that the subject of the first example (*goldfish*) is a noun. The verb (*died*) is an action verb.

The subject of the second example (*She*) is a pronoun. The verb (*is*) shows being.

"The subject is the person or thing you're talking about."

"The verb says something about the subject."

A. Draw one line under the subject and two lines under the verb.

1. **The dog barked at the stranger.**

2. The watch stopped at noon.

3. Joe was the winner of the race.

4. Someone dented our fender.

5. Our team defeated the champions.

6. Two apples are enough for my lunch.

7. Gold is a yellow metal.

8. The wind blew the lid off the garbage can.

9. A frog has bulging eyes.

10. They were busy all evening.

B. Write sentences about something you like to do. Draw one line under each subject (noun or pronoun). Draw two lines under each verb (action or being).

1. _____

_____

2. _____

_____

3. _____

_____

Time Out

Can you find the words that belong in these sentences? They are all nouns. Just fit the right letters between the letters that are given!

1. A person who cooks in a restaurant is a **C __ __F.**

2. A bad dream is a **N __ __ __ __ __ __ __E.**

3. Cows are milked at a **D __ __.__Y.**

4. Grass is cut with a **M __ __ __R.**

5. The winner of the race will get a gold **M __ __ __L.**

2. Diagramming the Subject and the Verb

A diagram explains something. It makes something easier to understand. Sentences can be diagrammed. A sentence diagram gives us a clear picture of how words are related to one another.

We will begin our study by diagramming the subject and the verb of this short sentence:

The crowd cheered.

STEP 1. Draw a horizontal line (base line). Then draw a vertical line through the base line. Your diagram should look like this:

STEP 2. Write the subject to the left of the vertical line.

STEP 3. Write the verb to the right of the vertical line.

English, Plain and Simple

A. Now try your hand at diagramming the subject and the verb in each sentence below. Do not worry about the other words in the sentence. The first diagram is done for you.

1. Fred built a fire.

Fred	built

2. Sam is a good friend.

3. The swing broke.

4. I am in the library.

B. Diagram the subject and the complete verb in each of these sentences. Be sure to include the helping verb.

1. Anne will help you.

Anne	will help

2. We have won the race.

3. Dad will play golf.

4. The clock has stopped.

As we continue our study of grammar, we will enlarge upon the diagram. In time, we will be able to diagram every word of even long sentences.

3. Subject and Verb Agree in Number

Nouns and pronouns have **number.** The noun *bell*, for example, is singular in number because *bell* refers to only *one* thing. Likewise, the pronoun *she* is singular because *she* refers to only *one* person.

The words *bell* and *she* can be used as subjects, as in these sentences:

> EXAMPLE 1: The bell rings every hour.
>
> > (Both the subject bell and the verb rings are singular in number.)
>
> EXAMPLE 2: She likes typing.
>
> > (Both the subject and the verb are singular.)

What do you notice about the verbs that are used with *singular* subjects?

A. Fill the blank with the verb that agrees with the subject.

1. (burn, burns)   The fire _____ brightly.

2. (play, plays)   Our school team _____ every Saturday.

3. (wait, waits)   Hal usually _____ on this corner for the bus.

4. (want, wants)   Lois _____ to be a nurse.

5. (run, runs)   The son _____ the family business.

So much for the singular! Now let's examine plural number.

> EXAMPLE 3: The bells ring every hour.
>
> > (Both the subject bells and the verb ring are plural.)
>
> EXAMPLE 4: We like typing.
>
> > (Both the subject and the verb are plural.)

What do you notice about the verbs that are used with *plural* subjects?

English, Plain and Simple   53

B. Fill the blank with the verb that agrees with the subject.

1. (mow, mows)   We _____ the lawn every other week.

2. (work, works)   They _____ together on the school newspaper.

3. (like, likes)   Elephants _____ peanuts.

4. (tell, tells)   Should we _____ Mother our holiday plan?

5. (hurt, hurts)   My fingers _____ from the frost.

So far, we have studied subjects that consist of only one noun or pronoun. But subjects can contain two or even more. In such a case, what happens to the verb?

Marty <u>plays</u> football.

George <u>plays</u> football.

Marty and George <u>play</u> football.

C. Fill in the blank with the verb that agrees with the subject. Be careful. Some sentences require a singular verb; others a plural verb.

1. (ride, rides)   Pat and Bud _____ the bus to school.

2. (find, finds)   Scientists _____ the truths about nature.

3. (giggle, giggles)   Joan _____ all the time.

4. (stop, stops)   My brother and sister _____ fighting when Father comes into the room.

5. (write, writes)   Penny and Sam _____ letters to each other.

6. (open, opens)   The janitor _____ the doors at 7 o'clock.

7. (make, makes)   Beverly and I _____ a good tennis pair.

8. (need, needs)   The dogs _____ fresh air and exercise.

9. (sing, sings)   She _____ the most songs in the musical.

10. (take, takes)   He and I _____ long walks on Sundays.

4. Agreement With the Verb Be

The singular and plural forms of *action verbs* change only slightly, as we have learned. The singular ends in s.

SINGULAR	PLURAL
The bell rings.	The bells ring.
The boy plays.	The boys play.
The girl sings.	The girls sing.

But the singular and plural forms of the verb *be* are quite different, as you will notice below.

SINGULAR	PLURAL
Our teacher is absent.	Our teachers are absent.
Our teacher was absent.	Our teachers were absent.

Be sure to use the proper verb to agree with its pronoun. Certain pronouns are singular, some plural.

SINGULAR PRONOUNS: *I, you, he, she, it*

PLURAL PRONOUNS: *we, you, they*

Examples:

(singular) I am tired.   (plural) We are tired.

He is tired.   You are tired.

She was tired.   They were tired.

English, Plain and Simple

A. Complete each sentence with the correct form of the verb *to be*. They are *am*, *is*, *are*, *was*, and *were*.

1. I _____ older than my brother.

2. She _____ here yesterday.

3. They _____ tired when they finished the race.

4. Henry _____ going to speak now.

5. Hamsters _____ nice pets.

6. You _____ upset with me last week.

7. Earlier this morning Eva _____ at the garage sale.

8. This mountain path _____ too steep.

9. What country _____ our southern neighbor?

10. Let's not swim until the waves _____ calm.

REMEMBER: When the subject consists of two or more nouns or pronouns joined by *and*, you should use a plural verb.

Michael is going to the planetarium.

Nicholas is going to the planetarium.

Michael and Nicholas are going to the planetarium.

B. Use the correct verb form in each of these sentences.

1. (is, are)   Cats and dogs _____ welcome in these apartments.

2. (is, are)   Cotton and barley _____ grown in this area.

3. (was, were)   Chris and Cathy _____ on time today.

4. (was, were)   Too much rain and too little sun _____ ruining the crops.

5. (was, were)   Parsley and lettuce _____ the two things I forgot.

English, Plain and Simple

C. Using these subjects, write sentences of your own. Make sure your verb agrees with the subject.

1. He _____

2. They _____

3. My neighbor _____

4. Matt and Mike _____

5. Our cities _____

ALPHABET CODE

			E				J			

— — — E — — — — J — — — —
1 2 3 4 5 6 7 8 9 10 11 12 13

O — — — T — — — — — Z
14 15 16 17 18 19 20 21 22 23 24 25 26

Fill in the code above with the rest of the letters of the alphabet. Then use the code to find the answers to the questions below.

To get you started answering the first question, find the 13th letter in the code. Write it on the answer line. Then find the 20th letter and write it on the line. You have now written MT. (The period following 20 means that MT is an abbreviation.) Continue the same way until you discover the answer.

What is the highest mountain in the United States?
Answer: 13–20. 13-3-11-9-14-12-5-25 _____

What is the fastest animal known for running short distances?
Answer: 3-8-5-5-20-1-8 _____

Who painted the Mona Lisa?
Answer: 4-1 22-9-14-3-9 _____

What is an animal called that carries its babies in a pouch?
Answer: 13-1-18-19-21-16-9-1-12 _____

What are the main languages spoken in Belgium?
Answer: 6-12-5-13-9-19-8 and 6-18-5-14-3-8 _____

English, Plain and Simple

WRITE ON!

$\mathcal{J}$ j _____

$\mathcal{K}$ k _____

$\mathcal{L}$ l _____

_____

Joan _____

Kathy _____

_____

Lee _____

_____

jury _____

knife _____

_____

long _____

_____

English, Plain and Simple

5. Review

A. Underline the subject once and the verb twice in each of these sentences.

1. The patient called for the nurse.
2. The spaceship had flown around the earth several times.
3. My aunt gave me a book.
4. The fire engine dashed around the corner.
5. The snow has turned into slush.
6. I am lost in this large building.
7. The members are paying for the trip.
8. We have guessed the answer.
9. Mario and George are good athletes.
10. Nadine and I are collecting jazz records.

B. Diagram the subject and the verb in each of these sentences. Ignore the other words in the sentence.

1. He is visiting his grandfather.

2. Gold was discovered in California.

3. She set the clock on the table.

C. Write the correct verb form in each sentence.

1. (sit, sits)   Cynthia and Craig _____ in the back row.

2. (was, were)   I _____ home all night.

3. (was, were)   They _____ ready to start the race.

4. (grow, grows)   The grass _____ fast after heavy rains.

5. (pass, passes)   Two trains _____ by my house.

6. (is, are)   Breakfast and dinner _____ our biggest meals.

7. (was, were)   Donna and Fred _____ in the first group.

8. (is, are)   Mr. Landau and his partner _____ buying a small computer.

9. (is, are)   Sam and Joe _____ working at King's Market.

10. (give, gives)   School vacations _____ us a chance to travel.

Try your hand at unscrambling these letters to spell a noun.

1. bgrrhuame (food)   _____

2. viemo (entertainment)   _____

3. meho (place)   _____

4. hcchru (place)   _____

5. pcelin (object used in school)   _____

6. tsrhi (clothing)   _____

7. namlopice (person)   _____

8. tudyaSra (day)   _____

9. tSbeepmre (month)   _____

10. ggnivhiaknsT (holiday)   _____

                            English, Plain and Simple

chapter five

1. A Look at Adjectives

> An *adjective* is a word used to modify (tell something about) a noun.
>
> **We live in a *brick* house.**
>
> *Brick* is an adjective which describes or modifies the noun *house. Brick* tells **what kind** of house.
>
> **Dad baked a *few* apples.**
>
> *Few* is an adjective modifying the noun *apples* by telling **how many**.

Many adjectives describe nouns by answering the question *What kind?* or *How many?*

A. An adjective is italicized in each sentence. Does it tell *what kind* or *how many?* Write the adjective in the correct column.

WHAT KIND?   HOW MANY?

_____   _____   1. Randy wore a *green* shirt.

_____   _____   2. It was a *sunny* day.

_____   _____   3. *Several* people are on line.

_____   _____   4. It was a *smooth* ride.

_____   _____   5. Maria had *many* friends.

> **A, *an*, and *the* are also adjectives. They belong to a special group called *articles*.**

B. Find the adjectives. Write each adjective in front of the noun it modifies. Include the articles *a*, *an*, and *the*.

1. Lena has red shoes with blue shoelaces.

   _____ shoes _____ shoelaces

2. Tired people filled the crowded bus.

   _____ people _____ _____ bus

3. She wanted a cold drink.

   _____ _____ drink

4. The driver delivered two small packages.

   _____ driver _____ _____ packages

C. Underline the adjectives (including articles) in each sentence.

1. They told an unbelievable story.
2. I ate a thick juicy steak.
3. We played on an old tennis court.
4. The husky man is a professional wrestler.
5. The American flag hangs in the classroom.

D. Choose an object in the room. Describe it in four or five sentences. Use as many adjectives as you can. Be sure each sentence has a subject and a verb as well as adjectives.

_____

_____

_____

_____

_____

2. Diagramming Adjectives

You know how to diagram subjects and verbs. (Look back to page 51.) In diagramming sentences having adjectives, notice that we place the adjective on a slanted line below the noun it modifies.

An angry bear growled at us.

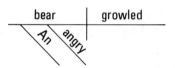

Diagram only the subject, verb, and adjectives in these sentences.

1. The glass vase is sold.

2. An atomic bomb was exploded.

3. One foreign student joined our class.

3. Using <u>A</u> and <u>An</u> Correctly

Both *a* and *an* are used before words that mean only *one*. Here are some important things to know about the use of *a* and *an*.

> **(1) Use *a* before words beginning with a consonant that is sounded.**
>
> EXAMPLE: a cat
>
> **(2) Use *a* before words beginning with the long sound of *u*.**
>
> EXAMPLE: a university
>
> **(3) Use *an* before words beginning with *a*, *e*, *i*, *o*, and the short sound of *u*.**
>
> EXAMPLES: an apple, an uncle
>
> **(4) Use *an* before words beginning with silent *h*.**
>
> EXAMPLE: an hour

A. Write *a* or *an* in front of each word.

1. _____ gorilla
2. _____ football
3. _____ union
4. _____ unicorn
5. _____ Indian
6. _____ ocean
7. _____ UFO
8. _____ umbrella
9. _____ ape
10. _____ eagle
11. _____ honest man
12. _____ honor student

B. Insert *a* or *an* in these sentences.

1. Julia's mother baked _____ cherry pie for dinner.

2. Chris has _____ hobby of collecting stamps.

3. Sarah worked as _____ usher at the play.

4. He is _____ American citizen.

5. The security guard made _____ hourly check of the building.

6. She played _____ ukulele.

7. The Eskimo built _____ igloo.

Synonyms

> A **synonym** is a word that means the
> same, or almost the same, as another word.
>
> rich, wealthy
> strong, sturdy

Although synonyms can be other parts of speech, all the synonyms in this lesson are adjectives.

Choose a synonym from the list of adjectives on the right that will take the place of the adjective in parentheses. Write it in the blank.

1. Toni said that it was a (*dull*) _____
   movie.

2. A (*low-priced*) _____ tennis racket may not be a bargain.

3. Steve is very (*sad*) _____
   that his team lost.

4. It was a (*bad*) _____ accident.

5. Our (*tiny*) _____ dog
   barks loudly.

6. The (*noisy*) _____ class became quiet when a
   visitor entered.

7. The (*sick*) _____ student was taken to the nurse.

8. A (*famous*) _____ author spoke at our school.

9. Maria wore a (*pretty*) _____ new dress to the party.

10. China has a very (*big*) _____ population.

ADJECTIVES

ill
boring
beautiful
small
loud
unhappy
large
terrible
well-known
cheap

Using the Dictionary

> *Guide words* are words printed at the top of each dictionary page. They tell you what the first and last words on the page are. You can tell just by looking at the guide words if a word you are looking for is on that page.

On a dictionary page that has the guide words **CAKE** and **CARD**, you will find these words: *call, candle, car.* (These come after **CAKE** and before **CARD**.)

You will not find these words on that same page: *cab, cafe, cage.* (They come before **CAKE**.) Nor will you find these: *chief, cradle, cup.* (They come after **CARD**.)

A. Check the words that you would find on a dictionary page beginning with the guide word **HAND** and ending with the guide word **HANGAR**.

_____ 1. handsome   _____ 4. handy   _____ 7. heavy

_____ 2. happy   _____ 5. helpful   _____ 8. high

_____ 3. half-mast   _____ 6. handwork   _____ 9. habit

B. If you need more practice in putting words in order, alphabetize these adjectives. When the beginning letters are the same, alphabetize by the first letters that are different.

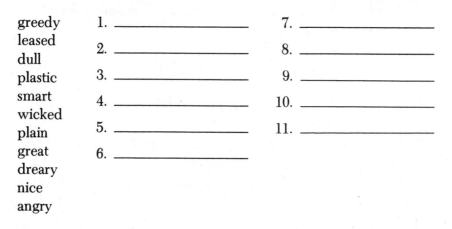

greedy   1. _____   7. _____

leased   2. _____   8. _____
dull

plastic   3. _____   9. _____

smart   4. _____   10. _____
wicked

plain   5. _____   11. _____

great   6. _____
dreary
nice
angry

4. Using <u>This</u>, <u>That</u>, <u>These</u>, and <u>Those</u>

The words *this*, *that*, *these*, and *those* are used to point out something about the nouns that follow them. They are adjectives that modify nouns by pointing out *which one* or *which ones*.

Use *this* or *that* with singular nouns. Use *these* or *those* with plural nouns.

SINGULAR

This apple is a good one.

That point did not count.

PLURAL

These books are new.

Those desks need washing.

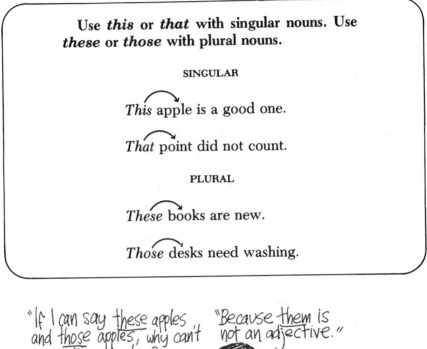

Which sentence in each pair sounds better?

This bike belongs to Jesse.
This here bike belongs to Jesse.

I like listening to that song.
I like listening to that there song.

You probably chose the first one in each pair. Why? The extra words *here* and *there* are not needed in the second sentences.

English, Plain and Simple

> Never say *this here, these here, that there, those there.*

A. Cross out the incorrect form.

1. (*That there, That*) man has been in line a long time.
2. He doesn't want any of (*those, those there*) magazines.
3. Is (*this, this here*) book yours?
4. Greg has never seen (*these, these here*) snapshots.
5. The teacher won't excuse anyone from (*this, this here*) test.
6. (*These, These here*) bushes stay green all year round.
7. I borrowed (*those, those there*) history notes from Carla.
8. (*That, That there*) kind of insect is very common in this area.
9. Do you like (*these, these here*) candies?
10. (*This, This here*) silver ring was bought in Mexico.

B. Write four sentences using the following adjectives correctly: *this, that, these, those.* Use each one before a noun.

1. _____

_____

2. _____

_____

3. _____

_____

4. _____

_____

5. Making Comparisons

When speaking of the height of three boys, you might describe one as *tall*, another as *taller*, and a third as the *tallest*.

---

(1) We often make comparisons by adding *er* or *est* to the root word.

rich, richer, richest

A. Following the model above, add endings to these words to show comparison.

1. quick _____ _____

2. bright _____ _____

3. smart _____ _____

4. young _____ _____

5. short _____ _____

---

(2) Words ending in *e* drop the *e* before adding *er* or *est*.

nice, nicer, nicest

B. Add the endings *er* and *est* to these words.

1. fine _____ _____

2. large _____ _____

3. white _____ _____

4. safe _____ _____

5. loose _____ _____

(3) **When the ending of a word has only one vowel followed by only one consonant, the consonant should be doubled before adding *er* or *est*.**

hot, hotter, hottest

C. Add the correct endings to these.

1. sad _____ _____

2. thin _____ _____

3. red _____ _____

4. wet _____ _____

5. fat _____ _____

(4) **We do not add *er* or *est* to an adjective that is long. Instead we put either *more* or *most* before it.**

beautiful, more beautiful, most beautiful

You may say	*You may NOT say*
√ more beautiful	Χ more beautifuller
√ most beautiful	Χ most beautifuller

D. Write the correct forms to show comparison.

1. skillful _____ _____

2. selfish _____ _____

3. exciting _____ _____

4. difficult _____ _____

5. interesting _____ _____

English, Plain and Simple

> **(5) When a word ends in *y*, the *y* must be changed to *i* before adding *er* or *est*.**
>
> happy, happier, happiest

E. Write the correct forms of these words.

1. pretty   _____   _____
2. shiny   _____   _____
3. sleepy   _____   _____
4. busy   _____   _____
5. funny   _____   _____

F. Write the correct form of the adjective in parentheses. Use the *er* or *more* method when comparing two people or things. Use the *est* or *most* method when comparing more than two.

1. **(brave)**   He is the _____ man I know.

2. **(tall)**   This is the _____ of the two houses.

3. **(difficult)**   Of all my school subjects, mathematics is the

    _____ _____ for me.

4. **(busy)**   Of the four workers, he is the _____.

5. **(harmful)**   Is overeating _____ _____ than undereating?

6. **(helpful)**   Jane's idea was the _____ _____ of all.

7. **(large)**   Alaska is _____ in size than Texas.

8. **(hot)**   Was April _____ than May?

9. **(easy)**   That was the _____ test I've ever taken.

10. **(thin)**   She is the _____ girl on the team.

WRITE ON!

M m _____

N n _____

O o _____

Mike _____

Nancy _____

Otis _____

man _____

none _____

off _____

6. Review

A. An adjective is a word that _____ a _____ .

B. Think of three adjectives that can describe the *wind*.

_____ _____ _____

C. Name the three articles. _____ _____ _____

D. Diagram the subject, verb, and adjectives in each sentence.

1. An awful noise was heard.

2. Many new plays are enjoying success.

3. That old creaky chair collapsed.

E. Draw lines to connect the synonyms in these lists.

rich	beautiful
ill	sick
noisy	sturdy
strong	loud
lovely	wealthy

F. Using these six adjectives, complete the sentences below.

brave	dangerous
red	expensive
several	worried

1. Hunters usually wear a _____ hat.

2. It is a _____ person who will go down the _____ rapids on a raft.

3. An _____ house is one that costs a lot of money to build.

4. The Mississippi River has _____ branches.

5. The _____ mother could not sleep because her son hadn't come home yet.

How many words of at least three letters can you make by re-shuffling the letters in CATASTROPHE? If you find 20, that's very good. We'll give you a couple to get you started.

CATASTROPHE

cat   _____

star   _____

_____   _____

_____   _____

_____   _____

_____   _____

_____   _____

_____   _____

_____   _____

G. Using your dictionary, find a synonym for each adjective below. (Remember what you have learned about guide words to make the finding of words in the dictionary easier.)

1. agile   _____
2. diligent   _____
3. genial   _____
4. solicitous   _____
5. tolerant   _____

H. Cross out the incorrect form.

1. (*That there, That*) man looks familiar.
2. Do you want any of (*this, this here*) soup?
3. (*Those, Them*) oranges look spoiled.
4. I can't get (*these here, these*) ropes untangled.
5. Copy all (*them, those*) problems from the board.

I. Use the correct form of the adjective on the left in each blank.

(healthy)

1. I would like to be a _____ person.

2. He is _____ than his cousin.

3. People who diet sensibly are the _____ of all.

(beautiful)

4. It was a _____ day.

5. Jerry thinks mountains are _____ _____ than valleys.

6. He chose the _____ _____ of all vacation spots.

(sad)

7. Marko is a _____ clown with drooping eyebrows.

8. He has a _____ look than his partner.

9. He is the _____ clown I have ever seen.

chapter six

1. How Adverbs Work

An adverb, like an adjective, is a modifier. Whereas an adjective modifies a noun, an adverb modifies a verb.

ADJECTIVE: We made an *early* start.
                                        N.

ADVERB: We started *early*.
                          V.

> An **adverb** is a word that modifies (tells something about) a verb. It answers the question *How? When?* or *Where?*
>
>   flew *fast*   (How?)
>   flew *later* (When?)
>   flew *away*   (Where?)

A <u>small</u> <u>log</u> cabin
  ADJ.   ADJ.

was nestled <u>peacefully</u>
                ADV.

in the <u>wooded</u> hills.
          ADJ.

A. Below are three pairs of sentences. The first of each pair contains an adverb. It is underlined. Using that model sentence, rewrite the second sentence to include an adverb. You may select an adverb from this list or use an adverb of your own.

hurriedly	already	there
late	slowly	early
always	here	inside

1. MODEL: (How?)   Dotty played her record player <u>loudly</u>.
Larry ate supper.

YOURS: _____

2. MODEL: (When?)   Dotty <u>often</u> played her record player.
Larry ate supper.

YOURS: _____

3. MODEL: (Where?)   Dotty played her record player <u>upstairs</u>.
Larry ate supper.

YOURS: _____

B. Complete each sentence with an adverb that answers the question in parentheses.

1. (How?)   My little sister screamed _____.
2. (When?)   I _____ swim in the afternoon.
3. (How?)   His father works _____.
4. (Where?)   Don't stand there. Come _____.
5. (When?)   They will come _____.
6. (Where?)   He ran. He stumbled. He fell _____.

In exercises A and B above, you have written adverbs ending in *ly*. Look back to your answers to *how*. Adverbs ending in *ly* are often made by adding *ly* to adjectives, which is the purpose of the next exercise.

C. On the left is an adjective and the noun it modifies. The adjective is italicized. At the right is a verb. You are to supply an adverb formed by adding *ly* to the adjective on the same line. Each adverb will answer the question *how?*

ADJECTIVE	ADVERB
loud noise	yelled __loudly__
1. *sudden* movement	left _____
2. *quick* stop	finished _____
3. *careful* hunter	planned _____
4. *dangerous* animal	lived _____
5. *strange* person	spoke _____
6. *eager* beaver	agreed _____
7. *exact* size	measured _____
8. *rapid* waterfall	flowed _____

D. There are ten adverbs in the paragraphs below. Find each adverb and draw a circle around it.

Jesse and his dad will soon take a backpack trip. They are eagerly awaiting the first day of the trip and have already bought the supplies they need. Jesse can easily carry a 30-pound pack of supplies. His father can certainly carry the rest.

Though they have planned the trip carefully, both of them are slightly worried about bad weather. They are checking the weather reports daily.

On the trip Jesse and his dad will stop frequently to fish and to take snapshots of wildlife. If all goes well, it will be a lot of fun.

English, Plain and Simple

2. Diagramming Adverbs

With each new part of speech you study, you will learn more about sentences and add to your diagramming skill. Now it is time to learn how adverbs are diagrammed. Let us work with this sentence.

The strong man <u>easily</u> bent the bar.

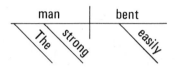

An adverb is placed below the word it modifies. In this example, the adverb *easily* modifies the verb *bent*.

Follow the model and diagram the subject, verb, adjectives, and adverb.

1. The model airplane barely flew.

2. One infant child slept peacefully.

3. A tiny bird was perched dangerously.

Reviewing Synonyms, Antonyms, Homonyms

> **Synonyms** are words with similar meanings.
>
> **Antonyms** are words with opposite meanings.
>
> **Homonyms** are words that sound alike but differ in spelling and meaning.

Study the pairs of words below. If the words in a pair are *synonyms*, write S. If they are *antonyms*, write A. And if they are *homonyms*, write H.

_____ 1.   dear   deer

_____ 2.   old   young

_____ 3.   finish   end

_____ 4.   sick   well

_____ 5.   brake   break

_____ 6.   light   dark

_____ 7.   happy   sad

_____ 8.   blue   blew

_____ 9.   pretty   beautiful

_____ 10. slowly   quickly

_____ 11. weak   week

_____ 12. be   bee

_____ 13. cord   rope

_____ 14. crooked   straight

_____ 15. present   gift

3. The Adverb Not

There is a special adverb that is used often. It is the word *not*. In a sentence having a helping verb, *not* is placed between the helping verb and the main verb. (Turn back to page 38 for a review of helping verbs.)

I will *not* be at school today.
H.V.   M.V.

(*Not* modifies the complete verb *will be*.)

A. In these sentences, draw an arrow from *not* to each verb it modifies.

    EXAMPLE: I will *not* go.

1. Bruce is not playing football this year.

2. Marion will not be here today.

3. I can not help you with your composition.

4. Some people do not own cars.

5. Angie may not pass.

Not is diagrammed like any other adverb—under the verb it modifies.

Roger did <u>not</u> win.

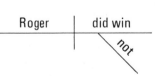

Contractions With <u>Not</u>

Remember: A **contraction** is made by joining two words and leaving out one or more letters. An apostrophe is used to take the place of the letter or letters that have been left out.

Many contractions are made by adding *not* to a verb.

A. In Group A, write the words from which the contraction is made. In Group B, write the contraction for the two words given.

GROUP A

1. aren't   _____   _____

2. can't   _____   _____

3. couldn't   _____   _____

4. wasn't   _____   _____

5. shouldn't   _____   _____

GROUP B

6. is not   _____

7. have not   _____

8. had not   _____

9. would not   _____

10. do not   _____

Bonus: This one is different. Do you know the two words from which this contraction is made? WON'T _____.

In diagramming contractions, you must break up the contraction.

I didn't forget.

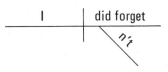

B. Diagram these "not" sentences.

1. Denise will not come.

2. The driver couldn't see clearly.

4. Avoiding Double Negatives

(1) **Negative** means "no." *No* and *not* are the most common negative words. There are other negative words that contain *no* and *not* within them:

none, nobody, nowhere, nothing, cannot

We can, of course, correctly use one negative word in a sentence, but we must not use two. If we do, we have what is called a *double negative*.

Larry does *not* have *no* time to study.	(Wrong)
Larry does not have time to study.	**(Right)**
Carla cannot go nowhere this afternoon.	(Wrong)
Carla cannot go anywhere this afternoon.	**(Right)**

or

Carla can go nowhere this afternoon.	**(Right)**

A. Rewrite these sentences to avoid the double negative. One will do the job!

1. I will not say nothing to Tony about the surprise party.

   _____

2. Nobody wants to take none of the blame for the broken window.

   _____

3. We cannot fish nowhere in this state without a license.

   _____

(2) Four more negative words are *never, hardly, scarcely,* and *barely*.

We had *not hardly* left the house when the rain started.	(Wrong)
We had hardly left the house when the rain started.	**(Right)**
Have you *never* gone to *no* rodeo?	(Wrong)
Have you never gone to a rodeo?	**(Right)**

B.   Avoid these double negatives.

1. I was not barely able to hear the speaker.

_____

2. Never did I see no one kick a ball so far.

_____

3. You could not scarcely tell the twins apart.

_____

> (3) A double negative happens when a sentence contains both a negative word and a contraction of _not_.
>
> | | | |
> |---|---|---|
> | Luis did*n't* (did _not_) say _nothing_. | (Wrong) |
> | **Luis didn't say anything.** | (Right) |
> | _or_   **Luis said nothing.** | (Right) |
>
> You should*n't* (should _not_) lend your
> toothbrush to _no one_.   (Wrong)
> **You shouldn't lend your toothbrush
> to anyone.**   (Right)
> _or_   **You should lend your toothbrush to
> no one.**   (Right)

C.   Rewrite these sentences to remove one negative.

1. She wouldn't not listen to me.

_____

2. I can't never remember her phone number.

_____

3. After the race, one runner couldn't hardly walk.

_____

4. She doesn't have no change.

_____

5. Don't you want to go nowhere this afternoon?

_____

Using Your Dictionary

A dictionary contains a wealth of interesting information, as you will discover in this exercise.

First find the underlined word in the dictionary. Then answer the question in a sentence or two. The first question is answered for you.

1. **Do you have a <u>cerebrum</u>? If so, what do you use it for?**
   <u>Yes, I use it to think and reason.</u>

2. Is it good to be <u>parsimonious</u>? Why?

3. Why is a dog called a <u>carnivorous</u> animal?

4. What is the length of a <u>fathom</u>?

5. Where are your <u>bronchi</u> located?

6. You would be most likely to find a <u>Hindu</u> in what country?

7. Did you ever see an <u>apparition</u>? When?

8. In what state does the <u>Mississippi River</u> flow into the Gulf of Mexico?

9. What would you feed a <u>phoebe</u>?

10. What does the abbreviation <u>A.M.</u> stand for?

5. More About Adverbs

We have been working with adverbs that modify verbs. Now take a look at the other kinds of words adverbs can modify.

> **Adverbs can also modify adjectives.**
>
> That is a *very* big sundae!

In the sentence above, *very* is an adverb that modifies the adjective *big*.

A. Draw an arrow from the italicized adverb to the adjective that it modifies.

1. It was a *truly* difficult test.

2. She has *very* dark hair.

3. Our neighbor has a *rather* large lawn.

4. The pool has a *really* deep section.

5. Mr. Smith is a *somewhat* careless person.

> **Adverbs can also modify other adverbs.**
>
> He ran *quite* fast.

Quite is an adverb that modifies another adverb—*fast*.

B. Draw an arrow from each italicized adverb to the adverb that it modifies.

1. Mark drives *terribly* fast.

2. Sandy writes *unusually* well.

3. She walked *rather* slowly.

4. Cheryl talks *too* much.

5. They tried *awfully* hard.

English, Plain and Simple

C. Draw an arrow from each italicized adverb to the word it modifies. Tell whether the word that is modified is an adjective or an adverb.

1. It happened *rather* suddenly.   <u> adverb </u>

2. He is a *really* great guy.   _____

3. She studied *extremely* late.   _____

4. They sing *somewhat* loudly.   _____

5. We formed a *rather* good team.   _____

6. They swam *very* well.   _____

Here is how you diagram an adverb that modifies an adjective or another adverb.

ADVERB MODIFYING AN ADJECTIVE:

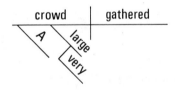

A very large crowd gathered.

ADVERB MODIFYING ANOTHER ADVERB:

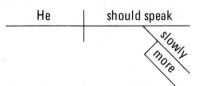

He should speak more slowly.

English, Plain and Simple

D. Diagram the following sentences.

1. An extremely brave firefighter perished.

2. Mr. Anthony calls very often.

The Paragraph

A writer expresses an idea, or tells a story, in a group of sentences called a *paragraph.* The number of sentences in a paragraph varies. It may consist of three or four or five sentences. This paragraph which you are now reading, for instance, is made up of five sentences. They tell you what a paragraph is.

All sentences in a paragraph are related to one another in a way that moves an idea along from beginning to end. The idea may be stated in one sentence, called the *topic sentence.* And all the other sentences will deal with that topic by giving details or information.

In the following paragraph, for example, the first sentence is the topic sentence. It tells us what the paragraph is about. It lets us know that Jesse had a bad day yesterday. The rest of the paragraph tells us why his day was bad. Read it and find out why.

1.

Jesse would like to forget all about yesterday. He got up late and missed his bus. When he finally got to school, his locker jammed, and he was tardy to his first class. In the cafeteria he dropped his tray. When he got to science class, he realized he had forgotten his homework, and so his grade was lowered. When the last bell rang, Jesse was ready to call it a day!

A. Then read paragraphs 2 and 3. Notice that each begins with a topic sentence and is followed with details.

2.

Jesse's friend Mario likes to play golf. Mario plays every chance he gets. Yesterday he played 18 holes and had a score of 96. He was lucky on one green and chipped in for an eagle. When he gets to high school, he will join the golf team. After he graduates, he may become a golf pro.

3.

The carnival that is coming to town has a new ride called "Whing Ding." It spins you around and turns you upside down while going very fast. Some people think it is scary, but exciting. Others just get sick.

B. The topic sentence isn't always the first sentence. Can you tell which one it is in this paragraph?

4.

Tropical fish come in a great variety of shapes, sizes, and colors. They have fascinating ways of moving, feeding, and breeding. The tank in which they live can be an attractive feature of any room. Tropical fish need far less care than dogs or cats. These are a few of the reasons why I recommend tropical fish as an excellent hobby.

C. Think of an object that you would like to invent. Describe it in a paragraph of at least four sentences. Underline your topic sentence.

Here is an example of a descriptive paragraph to help you.

I would like to invent a special pencil. It would contain a tiny transistor radio, and I could listen to music during class. A secret compartment would be built in for messages to my friends. The pencil would be self-correcting so that I would never have to worry about spelling or math again!

Now you try it.

_____

_____

_____

_____

_____

_____

_____

_____

_____

_____

_____

_____

_____

_____

_____

_____

_____

English, Plain and Simple

WRITE ON!

P p _____

_____

2 q _____

_____

R r _____

_____

Pat _____

_____

Quincy _____

_____

Rick _____

_____

penny _____

_____

quiet _____

_____

ran _____

_____

6. Review

A. Complete this sentence: An adverb _____
a verb by answering the question _____, _____,
or _____.
An adverb can also modify an _____ or
another _____.

B. Underline the adverbs in these sentences.

1. My mother spoke very quietly.
2. The corn is not planted there.
3. They seldom see their cousins.
4. Ice cream melts quickly at room temperature.
5. The sun always sets in the west.
6. My uncle does not need your truck.
7. He moved rather suddenly.
8. A monkey will never refuse a banana.
9. My dog can't eat here.
10. The kite flew very high.

C. Complete each sentence with an adverb that answers the
question *How? When?* or *Where?*

1. (When?)   The family moved _____.
2. (How?)   Luis gave his report _____.
3. (Where?)   Is the elevator going _____?

D. Diagram all the words in these sentences.

1. They aren't coming.

English, Plain and Simple

2. Two very tall men were seen here.

3. The poster is not hanging straight.

4. Sonja sings very well.

E. Correct these sentences by rewriting them.

1. We can't do nothing about it now.

   _____

2. None of the girls didn't want to go alone.

   _____

3. Nobody wouldn't help us.

   _____

4. I can't hardly finish this sundae.

   _____

5. Mother asks that I never go nowhere for a long time unless
   I tell her.

   _____

F. Remember homonyms? Two words having the same sound but different meanings and spellings are *homonyms*. In this paragraph are some homonyms used incorrectly. Cross out the wrong word, and write the correct one above it. Follow the model. Find five more.

Some
~~Sum~~ of us went to a country fare. An exciting event was a horse

race. A peculiar thing happened. Suddenly a gust of wind blue

the long tale of one horse into the face of a rider. He was blind for

a moment, and his horse stopped short as though it had breaks on

its hooves. Off the horse flew the rider. He wasn't hurt, but he

wasn't to happy either.

G. Underline the topic sentence in the following paragraph.

There is a person at our school whose job is helping the

students, the teachers, and the principal. Daily, he cleans the

rooms and takes care of the grounds. Also, he makes sure the

gym equipment is in good condition. He often helps prepare

for special events. This important person is Mr. Ferguson,

the janitor.

Time Out

All the vowels have been left out of these "super" adjectives. Can you put them back in?

1. S__NS__T__ __N__L   4. M__GN__F__C__NT
2. T__RR__F__C   5. __ __TST__ND__NG
3. BR__LL__ __NT   6. R__M__RK__BL__

chapter seven

1. The Nature of Prepositions

> A *preposition* is a word that joins a noun
> or pronoun to another word in a sentence.
>
> Here are some of the most common
> prepositions.
>
> | | | |
> |---|---|---|
> | after | for | on |
> | at | from | to |
> | before | in | up |
> | by | of | with |

A. Underline the prepositions in these sentences.

1. Al was in the play.

2. Sam arrived on time.

3. After lunch, he went home.

4. Nora received a package from me.

5. They waited by the gate.

6. They will buy the tickets at the game.

7. Will you please go for some ice cream?

8. Feed your dog before dinner.

9. Up the stairs they climbed.

10. Fish is an important source of food.

Here are the prepositions you have just studied, along with other common ones. Become familiar with this list.

PREPOSITIONS

about	beyond	out
above	by	outside
across	down	over
after	during	through
against	except	to
along	for	toward
among	from	under
around	in	underneath
at	inside	until
before	into	up
behind	like	upon
below	near	with
beneath	of	within
beside	off	without
between	on	

B. Complete each sentence with a preposition that fits the meaning of the sentence. Try to use as many different prepositions as you can.

1. The shoes _____ the floor need polish.

2. We moved _____ the house next door.

3. I left the house _____ an umbrella; I got soaked.

4. We rowed _____ the lake to get to the other side.

5. I found my glasses _____ the couch.

6. My sister was _____ the hospital for a short time.

7. The meeting will end _____ lunch.

8. We were losing _____ the fourth quarter.

9. She hid _____ the table.

10. He got a pool table _____ his birthday.

English, Plain and Simple

2. Prepositional Phrases

A prepositional phrase is a group of words. For example,

in the back row

The phrase begins with the preposition *in*. It ends with the noun *row*.

Here is another example, too easy to explain.

for him

DEFINITION: A *prepositional phrase* is a group of words that begins with a preposition and ends with a noun or pronoun.

A. Using these prepositions, write phrases of your own.

1. in _____ 4. beside _____

2. on _____ 5. at _____

3. under _____ 6. above _____

B. In these sentences, put parentheses around each phrase. Underline the preposition once. Double underline the noun or pronoun that ends the phrase. *Beware!* A sentence may have more than one prepositional phrase.

1. **Put the key (<u>under</u> the <u>mat</u>) (<u>for</u> <u>Manuel</u>).**

2. In 1939 German troops marched into Poland.

3. A man from the college spoke to our class about education.

4. Beside the garage were the prettiest trees.

5. The bus waited for me at the corner.

6. Under his coat Mike carried the small puppy.

7. The ball flew over us.

8. The road to the park is washed out.

English, Plain and Simple   97

9. They passed through the crowded hallway.

10. The President of the United States spoke to the people on TV last night.

CHECK UP: Do the prepositional phrases you have just marked begin with a preposition and end with a noun or pronoun? They should!

C. For each phrase in the list on the left, there is a phrase on the right that means the opposite. Draw a line to connect each pair.

1. up the hill   *a.* on the bottom

2. on the ground   *b.* above the surface

3. at the top   *c.* down the mountain

4. under the water   *d.* after graduation

5. during school   *e.* in the air

"Now, more about phrases..."

3. Adjective and Adverb Phrases

(1) A prepositional phrase may modify a *noun*. Do you recall that the modifier of a noun is an *adjective*? **Therefore, a phrase that modifies a noun is an *adjective phrase.***

The *boy* (with my brother) is our star player.
noun

The preposition *with* joins the phrase to the noun *boy*. The phrase *with my brother* tells something about *boy* by pointing out *which* boy. It does the work of an adjective that answers the question *Which one?*

> (2) A prepositional phrase may also modify a *verb*. What modifies a verb? An *adverb!* **So a phrase that acts like an adverb is an *adverb phrase.***
>
> I *studied* (in my room) all evening.
>   verb

The preposition *in* joins the phrase to the verb. The words *in my room* modify the verb *studied*. They do the work of an adverb by answering the question *Where?* I studied *where?—in my room.*

A. Put parentheses around each prepositional phrase. Draw an arrow from the preposition to the word that the phrase modifies. Then, in the blank, identify the phrase. Write *adjective phrase* or *adverb phrase.*

1. We moved across the street. _____

2. The bike in the rack is mine. _____

3. The ball rolled toward him. _____

4. We ran around the block. _____

5. The girl near him is my cousin. _____

6. At noon, the delivery truck arrived. _____

7. They went inside the gym. _____

8. A fight started between the teams. _____

9. Beside the coach stood the umpire. _____

10. The plant by the window needs water. _____

B. Write your own prepositional phrase for each sentence.

1. The ball bounced _____.

2. The bird _____ is a robin.

3. The food _____ looks delicious.

4. He walked _____.

5. The car parked _____ is Mother's.

English, Plain and Simple

4. Diagramming Prepositional Phrases

Study these two diagrams.

1. The wall around the house cracked.

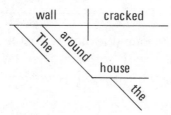

Around the house is a prepositional phrase that modifies the noun *wall*. It tells *which* wall. Therefore, the phrase acts as an adjective.

2. The gate was closed by the guard.

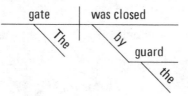

By the guard is a prepositional phrase modifying the verb *was closed*. It tells *how* the gate was closed. Therefore, this phrase does the work of an adverb.

3. One dog stayed at the edge of the pool.

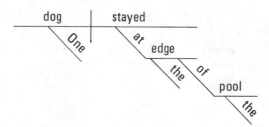

At the edge is a prepositional phrase modifying the verb *stayed*. A second phrase, *of the pool*, modifies the noun *edge*.

Diagram these sentences.

1. The thief ran down the street.

2. Whispers of the trapped men were heard.

3. A little girl walked beside the woman with the package.

5. Pronouns After Prepositions

As we have seen, a prepositional phrase begins with a preposition and ends with a noun or a pronoun. A noun at the end of a phrase causes no problem, but a pronoun does. How? We must be careful to use its correct form.

> **Use these pronouns after a preposition:**
>
> **me   him   her   us   them**
>
> We can say *with me* but not *with I*.
> We can say *to him* but not *to he*.

Observe the correct pronouns in these sentences.

> Please return the book (to *me*).
> I took a walk (with *him*).
> Did you prepare a sandwich (for *her*)?
> A bird flew (near *us*).
> (Between *them*) sat a young child.

Write the correct pronoun in each sentence.

1. The teacher was speaking to _____.
   I or me?

2. The letter is from _____.
   she or her?

3. The ball is bouncing toward _____.
   he or him?

4. Are you going with _____?
   they or them?

5. She looked for _____.
   we or us?

"This is important! Make sure you understand it."

The Friendly Letter

You are going to write a letter to a friend or relative. But first read Henry's letter to his uncle.

Heading ⟶ 210 Park Street
Lemoore, CA 93245
March 30, 1981

Dear Uncle Harry, ⟵ Greeting

Body ⟶ Thanks for the fishing pole and reel you sent me for my birthday. You really surprised me!

I used the pole for the first time last weekend. Mom, Dad, and I went fishing in the Kings River. I caught four fish and one was a beauty! It put up such a fight, I almost fell into the river.

We are planning another fishing trip in a few weeks. If you're not busy, why don't you come up and go with us? Maybe you can give me a few pointers.

Closing ⟶ See you soon,
Signature ⟶ Henry

- Write naturally, as if you were talking.
- Write about what the other person will want to know.
- Write neatly.

Now you can begin your letter. Compose it on separate paper.

Begin with the *heading*. As you see, it includes your address and the date of the letter.

Use capital letters for the names of your street, city, and state. The month, too, should be capitalized. Notice how a comma separates the city and state, and another comma separates the day of the month and year.

Finish your letter with a friendly closing and with your signature.

Here's an example of the correct way to address an envelope.

Henry Lewis
210 Park Street
Lemoore, California 93245

Mr. Harry Lewis
2421 W. Canal
Alhambra, California 91800

Dictionary Skills

Most often, you refer to a dictionary for a word's pronunciation, definition, spelling, and part of speech. You will be surprised at some of the other information you can find in a dictionary. There are also pictures, maps, and diagrams.

A. Using your dictionary, look up the following words to see if there are pictures, maps, or diagrams. Write *yes* or *no* for each.

1. Great Lakes	_____	6. snail	_____
2. lungs	_____	7. heart	_____
3. Sphinx	_____	8. terrapin	_____
4. bulldog	_____	9. Parthenon	_____
5. flower	_____	10. chevron	_____

Words have several forms, like *bright, brightly, brightness*. As dictionaries do not list all forms separately, you may not find *brightly* or *brightness*. If so, look under the main entry *bright*.

Here are other words that are not usually listed separately. For each one, look under the main entry word.

flavored	(Look for the entry word *flavor*.)
educational	(Look for the entry word *education*.)
countries	(Look for the entry word *country*.)
avoidable	(Look for the entry word *avoid*.)

"Here's a handy time-saver!"

Looking for a word in the dictionary? One way is to turn pages and look up and down each page until you find the word you want. A quicker way is to use the *guide words* at the top of each dictionary page. If you have forgotten how to use these time-savers, turn back to page 66.

B. What is the entry word you would look for to find each of the following? In some cases, you may find the word just as it is. If so, rewrite the word without changing it.

1. helping   —————————

2. frozen   —————————

3. industrious —————————

4. knives   —————————

5. electrical   —————————

6. generosity —————————

7. figured   —————————

8. rapidly   —————————

9. leaves   —————————

10. recitation —————————

A word may have several different meanings. A dictionary gives them. Be sure you choose the right meaning for the way the word is used in a particular sentence.

C. Here is some practice for you. Using your dictionary, give the exact definition for the italicized word as it is used in the sentence.

1. The dress had a *bow* that tied in the back.

    DEFINITION: ——————————————————————————

2. Did you hear the door bell *ring?*

    DEFINITION: ——————————————————————————

3. The dog's *bark* frightened the child.

    DEFINITION: ——————————————————————————

4. He will *draw* a number for the prize.

    DEFINITION: ——————————————————————————

WRITE ON!

S *s* _____

T *t* _____

U *u* _____

Sam _____

Tom _____

Uncle _____

sent _____

trip _____

union _____

_____

6. Review

A. A preposition is a word that joins a _____ or

_____ to another word in a sentence.

B. Underline the prepositions in these sentences.

1. I will be there before noon.
2. The books on the table are mine.
3. Jamie raced toward the goal line.
4. The plane soared above the clouds.
5. He looked in the closet and under the bed.

C. Put parentheses around each phrase and underline the preposition.

1. The plane will be here within an hour.
2. The weather was beautiful after the storm.
3. Our cabin is off the main road near the lake.
4. Louise sat between the two boys.
5. "Buck" was hiding inside the garage near the door.

D. Fill in each blank with an interesting prepositional phrase.

1. Everyone _____ cheered and shouted.

2. _____ the team had a steak dinner.

3. She sells cosmetics _____.

4. The woman _____ was sad.

5. You must wait _____.

E. First, put parentheses around each prepositional phrase. Then underline the word that the phrase modifies. Finally, identify each phrase by writing *adjective* or *adverb*.

1. The class in the next room is noisy. _____

2. The snake crawled under a rock. _____

3. Jerry fell off his bicycle. _____

4. The vegetables grew among the flowers in the garden. _____

5. The road near the lake was flooded. _____

F. Diagram these sentences.

1. The snake was dangling from a limb.

2. The road to town is closed for repairs.

G. Write the correct pronoun in each blank.

1. They acted unfriendly toward _____.
   we or us?

2. She came with _____.
   they or them?

3. Mother talked to _____.
   he or him?

4. Are you riding with _____?
   I or me?

5. The award went to _____.
   she or her?

English, Plain and Simple   109

chapter eight

1. Definition

> A *conjunction* joins other words, like two nouns or two pronouns. *And, or,* and *but* are the most common conjunctions.
>
> 1. *Cathy* **and** *Paula* are sisters.
>   (Two nouns are joined by *and*.)
>
> 2. *He* **and** *I* played tennis.
>   (Two pronouns are joined by *and*.)
>
> 3. He spoke *hurriedly* **and** *angrily*.
>   (Two adverbs are joined by *and*.)
>
> 4. You may *run* **or** *walk*.
>   (Two verbs are joined by *or*.)
>
> 5. A *light* **but** *steady* rain fell.
>   (Two adjectives are joined by *but*.)

A. Underline the conjunctions in these sentences. Tell what kinds of words are joined.

1. Will you have cake or ice cream?   _____

2. The girls worked quickly but carelessly.   _____

3. They may write or call.   _____

4. Please give it to him or me.   _____

5. The old and stately mansion was for sale.   _____

A conjunction may also join phrases.

1. Gerald ran *down the street* and *into the house.*
2. You may find some dimes *on my desk* or *in my coat pocket.*

B. Underline the conjunction. Put parentheses around the prepositional phrases that are joined by the conjunction. The first sentence is done for you.

1. **Don't drop candy wrappers (on the street), <u>but</u> (into a waste-basket).**

2. Put the bread on the kitchen table or in the breadbasket.

3. The United States is strong on land, in the air, and on the sea.

4. Over TV and on radio we heard the glad news.

5. Twenty is under thirty, but over ten.

6. Sacramento in California and Harrisburg in Pennsylvania are capital cities.

C. Write a conjunction that fits the meaning of each sentence.

1. Dennis washed _____ polished the station wagon.

2. Liz bought a pretty _____ inexpensive dress.

3. Should we go to the movies _____ to the park?

4. The Tigers _____ the Bulldogs were tied for first place.

5. You will find Mr. Kosis in the gym _____ at the stadium.

2. Diagramming Conjunctions

How do we diagram sentences with conjunctions?

NOUNS: **Cathy and Paula** left later.

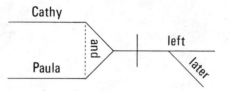

VERBS: **He tried but failed.**

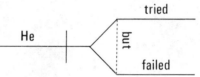

ADJECTIVES: **A light but steady rain was falling.**

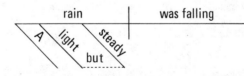

ADVERBS: **He spoke hurriedly and angrily.**

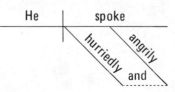

Diagram all the words in these sentences. You may look back for help if you need it.

1. The dog yawned and stretched.

2. Sally and I left early.

3. He whistled softly but clearly.

4. The pretty and talented girl easily won.

3. Using Pronouns in Compounds

> Two or more words that are joined by the conjunction *and, but,* or *or* form a **compound word group.**
>
> (Ann *and* she) are classmates.
> Mrs. Perez called upon (Alfred *but* not me).
> (Tom, Dick, *or* I) will mow the lawn.

When a pronoun is part of a compound word group, it is sometimes a problem to decide which form of the pronoun to use.

EXAMPLE: Mary and (_____) will clean up.
I or me?

Here is a method to help you decide which form is correct in the sentence above, *I* or *me*. First, read the sentence without the words *Mary and*. Then try each pronoun (*I* or *me*) with the rest of the sentence. Which sounds better?

I will clean up.   OR   *Me* will clean up.

Of course, you would not say, "Me will clean up." You would say, "I will clean up." It is correct, then, to say "Mary and I will clean up."

Try another one.

EXAMPLE: The teacher called on Randy and (_____).
he or him?

The teacher called on *him*.   OR   The teacher called on *he*.

Since it is correct to say, "The teacher called on him," it is also correct to say, "The teacher called on Randy and him."

Try these on your own. Fill in the blank with the correct pronoun.

1. _____ and Sandra entered the race.
   She or Her?

2. The championship contest was won by Paul and _____.
   he or him?

3. Peter and _____ want to earn some money.
   I or me?

4. Will Jim go with them or _____?
   we or us?

5. Patricia and _____ will be cheerleaders.
   they or them?

6. _____ or our neighbors will take care of your pets.
   We or Us?

7. Can _____ or Kathy drive to the airport?
   he or him?

8. Mrs. Clark asked my friends and _____ to meet after school.
   I or me?

English, Plain and Simple

9. The police worked together with Mark and _____.
they or *them?*

10. John and _____ helped move the furniture.
I or *me?*

4. Commas in Compounds

When three related words (like 3 nouns or 3 adjectives) are listed in a row, they need separation. A comma is inserted between them.

> Do you want *chocolate, marshmallow,* or *butterscotch* sauce on your ice cream?
> (3 nouns)

Note: The comma before the conjunction *or* is not really necessary. It is your choice to use it or not.

> The *tall, husky, red-haired* boy is Alfred.
> (3 adjectives)

Since there is no conjunction separating the second and third adjectives, each one must be set off with a comma.

Insert commas where they are needed in these sentences.

1. He wants records tapes and posters for his birthday.

2. Do you like catsup pickles and onion on your hamburger?

3. I invited Don Jeff Kathy and Helen to my party.

4. A doctor an accountant or a lawyer will move into the empty office.

5. You will find the fried chicken deviled eggs and tomatoes in the large picnic basket.

6. He spoke slowly carefully clearly.

Writing a Paragraph

Now that you have worked with conjunctions, try using them in a paragraph. In your paragraph, compare yourself with a close friend, brother, or sister.

Here is an example. Notice how the conjunctions *and, or,* and *but* are used to join words and word groups.

Two important people in a school are the principal **and** the student. You might think they are very different, **but** in many ways they are alike. The student wants fair rules, **and** so does the principal. Both want the school to be an enjoyable place. The student wants to learn, **and** the principal tries to see that he **or** she can. Most of all, both student **and** principal want what is best overall for the student.

Now, here is space for your paragraph. Be sure to include the conjunctions you have been working with.

CHECK UP: Did you indent?

Do you have a topic sentence?

Do you have three or four supporting sentences that give details?

English, Plain and Simple

Write On!

$\mathcal{V}$ v _____

_____

$\mathcal{W}$ w _____

_____

$\mathcal{X}$ x _____

_____

Vernon _____

_____

Wendy _____

_____

Xerox _____

_____

van _____

_____

won _____

_____

5. Review

A. What does a conjunction do in a sentence? _____

_____

B. Underline each conjunction. Put parentheses around the adjectives or adverbs that are joined by the conjunction.

1. Nina swam far but effortlessly.

2. The old and cranky man chased the kids away.

3. We have had a long and bitter winter.

4. Is yours a wood or brick house?

5. He was sleeping peacefully and soundly.

C. Underline each conjunction. Put parentheses around the phrases that are joined by the conjunction.

1. You may find her on the trail or in the cabin.

2. A farmer had seen coyote tracks near the sheep pen and behind the chicken coop.

3. He planted seeds around the trees and beside the fence.

4. The wind carried the kite over the rooftops and into the clouds.

5. Luke hit the ball above the center fielder's head but not over the fence.

D. Diagram these sentences.

1. Bob and José aren't going with us.

2. She listened quietly and patiently.

3. A small but valuable vase disappeared.

4. The tugboat chugged and puffed through the channel.

E. Write the correct pronoun in each sentence.

1. Carol and _____ want to go to the late show.
      I or me?

2. Will _____ and Linda work together?
      he or him?

3. The guides entered the cave with Wilma and _____.
                                              we or us?

4. The class elected Roy and _____.
                            I or me?

5. _____ and the other team had a close game.
   They or Them?

6. Carl and _____ did not see the movie.
            she or her?

7. We waited for Barbara and _____.
                              they or them?

8. Dad met Mom and _____ in the supermarket.
   she or *her?*

9. The bus driver gave Jerry and _____ the right directions.
   we or *us?*

10. The lifeguard taught Harry and _____ how to use a surfboard.
    I or *me?*

F. Put commas where they are needed in these sentences.

1. He likes water skiing swimming sailing and water polo.

2. Marcia joined the French Club the newspaper staff and the orchestra this year.

3. We are storing the bicycles baby carriages and shopping carts in the basement.

4. Linda Janet or I may baby-sit for Aunt Margaret on Saturday.

5. Peaches plums but not cherries are on sale today.

Fill the blanks with letters that spell a small word inside a larger word. Follow the model.

1. SCRA I CH   Put "a small animal that gnaws" inside "what you do when you itch."

2. G___ ___ ___ ___S   Put "what you feel when you like someone very much" inside "a pair of things you wear on your hands."

3. S___ ___ ___M   Put "what you call it when two countries are fighting" inside "a group of bees."

4. P___ ___ ___ER   Put "a beam of light" inside "a request made to God."

5. T___ ___ ___ER   Put "the last of something" inside "a word that means gentle."

6. S___ ___ ___D   Put "a light-brown color" inside "the opposite of sit."

chapter nine

1. Words That Show Feelings

Are you ready for the last of the eight parts of speech? This is one that you use when you are excited about something.

> An *interjection* is a word that is used to show sudden or strong feeling.
>
> Ouch!
> Oh!
> Stop!

Even ordinary words can be used as interjections if you intend them to show excitement, surprise, or any other strong feeling.

Place an interjection on the blank line before each sentence. Choose the one from those given below that best expresses the feeling shown in the sentence.

Beware!   Wait!   At last!   Welcome!   Nonsense!

1. _____ Vicious dog!

2. _____ The traffic light has turned red!

3. _____ I don't believe a word of it!

4. _____ It's nice to see you.

5. _____ I finally have enough money for it.

2. Mild Interjections

There are different levels of feeling.

EXAMPLES: *Hurray!* Our team won the championship!
Sorry, it couldn't be helped.

In the first example, strong feeling is expressed. Notice the exclamation mark after the interjection.

The second example shows a milder feeling. Notice that a comma follows the interjection, and the next word begins with a small letter.

A. Write an interjection for each of these sentences. Use a comma after the interjection to show that it expresses a mild feeling.

| Ah | My | Please | Shsh | Yes |

1. _____ you're so pretty.

2. _____ that feels good.

3. _____ may I go with you?

4. _____ I agree with you.

5. _____ don't say a word.

B. Using an interjection, write a sentence about each feeling that is expressed at the left.

1. (joy) _____

_____

2. (surprise) _____

_____

3. (anger) _____

_____

3. Diagramming Interjections

Interjections are diagrammed on a separate line to the left of the rest of the sentence diagram.

<u>Oh!</u> I almost lost.

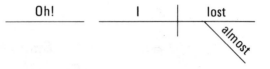

Diagram these sentences.

1. Ah! I guessed correctly!

2. Hurrah! My favorite team won!

3. Well, I may go with you.

English, Plain and Simple

The Business Letter

A business letter has a different purpose from a friendly letter. You write a friendly letter to get in touch with a friend or relative. It is a personal message. In a business letter, you write a company to order its product, to request information, or to complain about something. A business letter should be *brief, clear, polite, neat*.

Heading ——→ 415 Cameron Way
Lemoore, CA 93245
April 10, 1981

Disco Record Company
P.O. Box 3270 ←—— Inside Address
Houston, TX 77010

Dear Sir or Madam: ←—— Greeting

Body ——→ Please send me a list of the top fifty hits for this year. As I need the information, I hope you can send it soon. I have enclosed a stamped, self-addressed envelope for your quick reply.

Closing ——→ Yours truly,
Signature ——→ Mary Wells

English, Plain and Simple

In a business letter:

- Write your address, city, state, ZIP code, and the date in the *heading*.

- Write the name, address, city, state, and ZIP code of the company to whom you are writing. (*inside address*)

- Use a colon after the *greeting*.

- Make sure you give all the needed information in the *body* of the letter.

- End your letter with one of the following *closings*:

  Yours truly,   Very truly yours,
  Sincerely,   Sincerely yours,

Now write a business letter on separate paper. Use your own name and address and today's date. Order something, or ask for information, or complain about the company's service.

Address the envelope.

Mary Wells
415 Cameron Way
Lemoore, CA 93245

        Disco Record Company
        P.O. Box 3210
        Houston, TX 77010

WRITE ON!

Y *y* _____

_____

Z *z* _____

_____

Yangtze _____

_____

Zeus _____

_____

year _____

_____

zebra _____

_____

Congratulations!!!

You are now a graduate of THE SCHOOL OF PENMAN-
SHIP. The following certificate may be filled out by you and
signed by your teacher.

This is to certify that

Nate MANDLAOTI

has successfully completed the advanced course

in

THE SCHOOL OF PENMANSHIP

7-29-99

——————————————
Date

——————————————
Signature of Teacher

With
Honors

4. Review

A. What is an interjection? _____

_____

B. Insert one of these interjections in a sentence below. Make sure that your sentence makes sense and that you include the correct punctuation.

Hurrah   Ouch   No   Hey   Really

1. _____ I twisted my ankle!

2. _____ Wait for me!

3. _____ Here comes the parade!

4. _____ it has stopped raining!

5. _____ she won't believe your excuse.

C. Now that you know all the parts of speech, write the correct part of speech above each word in the following sentence.

Oh no! Jack and she nearly fell off the frightened horse!

chapter ten

1. What Is a Sentence?

In written English, we express our ideas in sentences. **A *sentence* is a group of words that expresses a complete thought.**

As you know, **every sentence has a *subject*.** The subject may be a noun or pronoun.

> *Nouns as Subjects:*
>> <u>Alice</u> prepared breakfast.
>> <u>New York</u> is a crowded city.
>> The <u>circus</u> came to town.

> *Pronouns as Subjects:*
>> <u>She</u> prepared breakfast.
>> <u>It</u> is a crowded city.

A sentence must also have a *verb*. The verb may be a single word, or a main verb and a helping verb.

> The pond <u>freezes</u> every winter. (one verb)
> Mary <u>has left</u> for school.   (main verb *left* + helping verb *has*)

> **Every sentence must have a *subject* and a *verb* and express a complete thought.**
>
>   S   V
> <u>Kerry</u> <u>lives</u> near me.

Add your own subjects or verbs, as the case may be, to complete these sentences.

1. The grass _____ tall.

2. _____ is my favorite season.

3. The _____ plowed his fields.

4. Tim _____ baseball.

5. Mario _____ his guitar.

6. The _____ is my favorite team.

7. Who _____ all of the ice cream?

8. _____ may arrive today.

9. Shawn _____ his dinner.

10. Greg _____ _____ here later.

2. The Subject of a Sentence

> The subject tells *who* or *what* about the verb.
>
> S V
> He ate the cake.
>
> (*He* is the subject. It tells *who* ate the cake.)
>
> S V
> The boat sank slowly.
>
> (*Boat* is the subject. It tells *what* sank.)

A. Underline the subject. Check whether the subject tells *who* or *what* about the verb. The first one is done for you.

	WHO	WHAT
1. **He hit a foul ball.**	✓	
2. The bus was crowded.		
3. A burglar stole our stereo.		
4. Karen needs a few days of rest.		

English, Plain and Simple

5. Our vacation will be fun.   _____ _____

6. They drank a gallon of ice tea.   _____ _____

7. My brother will go to U.C.L.A.   _____ _____

8. Condors are endangered birds.   _____ _____

9. The corn was ready to be harvested.   _____ _____

10. We are taking scuba-diving lessons.   _____ _____

The subject of a sentence usually comes before the verb, but not always. For instance, in questions, the verb, or part of the verb, often comes first.

Was he late?

Did Mary make her dress?

It is helpful to change a question to a statement to find the subject and the verb. Compare these statements with the above questions.

He was late.

Mary did make her dress.

B. Underline the subject once and the verb twice.

1. Was Robin hurt in the accident?

2. Will you drive to the beach?

3. Is she coming to the party?

4. Does the novel have a happy ending?

5. Were you the first person in line?

3. The Verb of a Sentence

> The verb tells of an action or a condition (being) of the subject.
>
> Peter lost his lunch money.   (action verb)
> The coach was late.   (being verb)

You may recall that, in Chapter 3, we studied verbs of *action* and *being*. For review, here is a list of being verbs. All are forms of the verb *be*.

am   are   were   being
is   was   be   been

A.   Draw two lines under the verb. Then write a check to show whether the verb expresses action or being.

	ACTION	BEING
1. An elderly woman <u>was</u> last in line.	_____	✓
2. Dad popped corn for everyone.	_____	_____
3. He chopped the tree down.	_____	_____
4. Martha is an expert swimmer.	_____	_____
5. I am the only lifeguard on duty.	_____	_____
6. We graded our own tests.	_____	_____
7. Did you miss the fourth quarter?	_____	_____
8. Boiling water changes to steam.	_____	_____
9. Bill and Donna are club members.	_____	_____
10. They were just being friendly.	_____	_____

B.   In these sentences about famous "D's," underline the subject once, the verb twice.

1. Dallas is called the "Big D."

2. Denver is the "Mile-High City."

3. The Danube is a great river in Europe.

4. Delaware ratified the Constitution before any other state.

5. Daniel was thrown into a den of lions.

6. Queen Elizabeth knighted Francis Drake.

7. Was Darius King of Persia?

8. Leonardo daVinci painted the *Mona Lisa*.

9. Jefferson Davis became the President of the Confederacy in 1861.

10. Is Death Valley in California or Nevada?

4. The Direct Object

Here is a word group with a subject (*FBI*) and a verb (*captured*). Yet it does not make complete sense.

The FBI captured . . .

By asking "WHOM did the FBI capture?" we get:

The FBI captured the *kidnapper*.

Kidnapper completes the meaning of the verb *captured*.

The following is another word group with a subject and verb. Does it express a complete thought? What does it lack?

Ed securely tied . . .

If we ask "WHAT did Ed tie?" we get:

Ed securely tied the *package*.

Package, the receiver of the action verb *tied*, is a **direct object**.

> A **direct object** completes the action of a verb. It names the receiver of the action by asking WHO? or WHAT? It may be a noun or a pronoun.

Underline the subject once and the verb twice. Then draw a circle around the direct object.

1. Muriel has visited the haunted house.
2. The noise frightened her.
3. He drives a white Jaguar.
4. Fred typed his composition.
5. Marcie has memorized the poem.
6. Ed is fixing the bike.
7. The dog chewed the bone.
8. Phil borrowed my math book.
9. Dad's boss will promote him.
10. She corrected the mistake.

English, Plain and Simple

5. Diagramming Direct Objects

Notice the vertical line between the verb (*flattened*) and the direct object (*house*). The vertical line touches the horizontal line but does not cross it.

The tornado flattened our <u>house</u>.

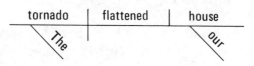

Diagram the following sentences.

1. We saved very few things.

2. Our kind neighbors helped us.

3. We will soon rebuild our cottage.

English, Plain and Simple

Prefixes

One way to improve your vocabulary is through a study of *prefixes*. A prefix appears at the beginning of a word.

> **(1) A prefix can change the meaning of a word.**
>
> legible (readable)   ILlegible (not readable)
>
> test (to examine)   PREtest (to examine before)
>
> **(2) A prefix can add to the meaning of a word.**
>
> port (to carry)   TRANSport (to carry across)
>
> fill (a full supply) REfill (a fresh supply)

Here are some common prefixes:

re-	(again)	dis-	
pre-	(before)	un-	
trans-	(across)	in-	
inter-	(between)	non-	(not)
mis-	(wrong)	im-	
semi-	(half)	il-	

A. Each word below begins with a prefix, as **dis** in the word *disagree*. If you refer to the list of prefixes above, you will find that **dis** means "not." Therefore, *disagree* means "not agree," as in the sentence "I disagree with Timmy."

Following the model, complete the exercise.

1. disagree not agree _____

2. rebuild _____

3. transcontinental _____

4. immovable _____

5. misplace _____

6. nonmembers _____

7. prehistoric _____

8. unsuitable _____

9. inactive _____

English, Plain and Simple   135

10. interstate _____

11. semicircle _____

12. illegal _____

B. You can shorten these sentences by adding a prefix to the underlined word and omitting one or more words. Not only will you have shorter sentences, but also stronger ones. Use this method in all your future writing.

1. John <u>judged</u> the new boy before they met.

   John prejudged the new boy.

2. This material is not <u>perfect</u>.

   _____

3. Would you please <u>read</u> that paragraph again?

   _____

4. Sara may <u>pronounce</u> that word wrong.

   _____

5. Smoking is not a <u>healthy</u> habit.

   _____

6. His flight was across the <u>Atlantic</u>.

   _____

7. Some diseases are not <u>communicable</u>.

   _____

8. They said the evidence was not <u>admissible</u>.

   _____

You have worked with just a few of the prefixes in our language, and some of these have meanings other than the ones given. A dictionary will be a lot of help in your study of prefixes. Once you are familiar with a number of them, you will be able to figure out the meanings of many unfamiliar words.

6. Review

A. Every sentence must have a _____ and a
_____ and express a _____ thought.

B. Underline the subject once, the verb twice.

1. Jason likes chocolate ice cream.

2. Were you surprised?

3. Vicki will speak at graduation.

4. In our garden, Joe planted roses.

5. Marla joined our club.

C. Underline the direct object (*D.O.*) in each sentence.

1. Rose visited me last night.

2. Ken broke his arm.

3. He swept the sidewalk.

4. The goalie stopped the puck.

5. Billy dropped the plate.

D. Here are some words with common prefixes. Use each one in a sentence.

1. preview _____

_____

2. misprint _____

_____

3. transoceanic _____

_____

4. disconnect _____

_____

5. semiprecious _____

_____

chapter eleven

1. Purposes of Sentences

You have just worked with three kinds of sentences: simple, compound, and complex. In this lesson, you will see that sentences can be classified in still another way. Sentences can be put together in groups according to their purpose.

Do you want to tell something?

Use a *declarative* sentence.

Do you want to ask something?

Use an *interrogative* sentence.

Do you want to give a command?

Use an *imperative* sentence.

Do you want to express strong feeling?

Use an *exclamatory* sentence.

The following are the four purposes of a sentence.

To make a statement:

A sentence that tells something ends with a period. It is called a ***declarative sentence.***

To ask a question:

A sentence that asks something ends with a question mark. It is called an ***interrogative sentence.***

EXAMPLES: Where is Alex?   (*Question*)
He went bowling.   (*Statement*)

Do you have a pet? (*Question*)
I have a bulldog.   (*Statement*)

A. In a full sentence, write either a statement or a question, as needed.

1. (*Question*)   What did you get for your birthday?

   (*Statement*) _____

2. (*Question*)   _____

   (*Statement*) I enjoy playing baseball.

3. (*Question*)   What other cities have you lived in?

   (*Statement*) _____

4. (*Question*)   _____

   (*Statement*) I intend to go to college.

5. (*Question*)   What do you like to do on weekends?

   (*Statement*) _____

Here are the two other kinds of sentences that you will need to know—the request (or command) and the exclamation.

> **To make a request or command:**
>
> A sentence that requests something or tells someone to do something ends with a period or an exclamation point. It is called an *imperative sentence.*
>
> **To express a strong feeling:**
>
> A sentence that expresses strong feeling ends with an exclamation point. It is called an *exclamatory sentence.*
>
> EXAMPLES: Please close the door.   (*Request*)
> What a great day this is!
> (*Exclamation*)

B. Write a request and an exclamation.

(*Request*) _____

(*Exclamation*) _____

C. Now practice with these two kinds of sentences by putting *R* or *E* before each sentence to tell its kind.

R—request   E—exclamation

1. _____ Please don't be late.

2. _____ How nice you look!

3. _____ What fun we had!

4. _____ Make a right on Elm Street.

5. _____ Say "hello" for me.

D. What are the purposes of these sentences? Classify them by letter.

S—statement   Q—question   R—request   E—exclamation

1. _____ Alfred told a joke.

2. _____ Tell another joke, Alfred.

3. _____ Where did you buy that shirt?

4. _____ What a crazy joke that was!

E. Punctuate these sentences correctly.

1. Please help me with these packages

2. What a narrow escape I had

3. Did Loretta lose all her money

4. Who's at the door

5. The doctor left for the hospital

2. Phrases and Clauses

Sentences are composed of words. Some words join closely to form prepositional phrases. Remember?

> PHRASE: Men <u>in blue uniforms</u> are police officers.

> PHRASE: More women are going <u>to college</u> today.

What is a *phrase?*

> A *phrase* is a group of words which has neither a subject nor a verb.
>
> EXAMPLE: The woman *in the store* is my mother.
>
> (In this prepositional phrase, is there a subject? Is there a verb? Each answer is *No!*)

A. For review, underline the prepositional phrases in the following sentences. Reread each phrase. Is there a subject or a verb in any of these phrases?

1. Tony looked behind the couch.

2. My best friend lives across the street.

3. The locker near mine is stuck.

4. Logs floated down the river.

5. Please set the vase on the table.

Another group of words is a *clause*.

> **A *clause* is a group of words which does contain a subject and a verb.**
>
> $$\text{He gave me the present } \underline{\overset{\text{S} \quad\ \text{V}}{\text{before he left the party}}}.$$

A clause differs from a phrase. A phrase does not have a subject and a verb, but a clause does.

Clause: <u>When the rain stopped</u>, the game continued.

SUBJECT: *rain*—VERB: *stopped*

Clause: Eat less sweets <u>if you want fewer cavities</u>.

SUBJECT: *you*—VERB: *want*

B. Each underlined group of words below is a clause. Put S above the subject and V above the verb.

1. Amy was glad <u>when the movie ended</u>.

2. The day <u>before we graduated</u> was hectic.

3. Mary will call us <u>if she can go</u>.

4. We will stay on the beach all morning <u>unless it rains</u>.

5. <u>Although the taxi was late</u>, they got to the airport on time.

Look back to the sentences in Exercise B, where you labeled the subject and verb of underlined clauses. Your answer to the first sentence should have been:

$$\text{Amy was glad } \underline{\overset{\text{S} \qquad\ \text{V}}{\text{when the movie ended}}}.$$

> Actually, there are two clauses in this sentence:
> $$\underset{\text{main clause}}{\underline{\overset{\text{S} \quad\ \text{V}}{\text{Amy was glad}}}} \quad \underset{\text{dependent clause}}{\underline{\overset{\text{S} \qquad\ \text{V}}{\text{when the movie ended}}}}.$$
>
> The main clause (*Amy was glad*) expresses a complete thought. The dependent clause (*when the movie ended*) does not make complete sense. The dependent clause needs the help of the main clause to be complete in meaning.

C. Label the main clause and the dependent clause in each sentence.

1. I'll wait in line while you buy the tickets.

2. As Alice unpacked the groceries, Jack put them away.

3. After the game ended, we went for snacks.

4. The family is not the same since the triplets were born.

3. Simple Sentences

There are three kinds of sentences according to their clauses.

Simple Sentence: has one main clause.

Compound Sentence: has two main clauses.

Complex Sentence: has one main clause and one dependent clause.

We will start our study with the *simple sentence*.

> A *simple sentence* consists of one subject and one verb that work together to express a complete thought.
>
>   S   V
> I packed five of those cartons.
>
>   S   V
> The rumble of trucks broke the silence.

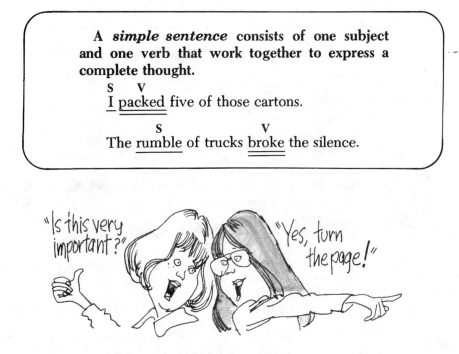

"Is this very important?"   "Yes, turn the page!"

If the word group below is a simple sentence, check the correct column. If it is not a sentence at all, check either the NO SUBJECT or NO VERB column to show what is missing. The first three groups are answered for you.

	Simple sentence	No subject	No verb
1. Was lonely.		✓	
2. The boy in the house.			✓
3. My eyes are green.	✓		
4. The telephone rang.			
5. Swam in the river.			
6. Ate everything.			
7. The old man in the sea.			
8. She cried.			
9. Ran fast.			
10. The little baby girl.			
11. Ran all the way home.			
12. We have a color TV.			
13. The car in the street.			
14. I shall study.			
15. Can't come.			
16. Sharon found her wallet.			

Note: We can say, in other words, that a simple sentence is *one* main clause.

4. Compound Sentences

> A *compound sentence* is made up of two main clauses joined by a conjunction: *and, but,* or *or*.
>
> (Ray hung the wallpaper), *and* (I painted the trim).
>
> (I knocked on the door), *but* (no one answered).
>
> (Vera must help us), *or* (we will not finish in time).

In the compound sentences above, notice two things: (1) The word group on each side of the conjunction contains a subject and a verb. Therefore, each is a *clause*. (2) Each clause expresses a complete thought. Therefore, each is a *main clause*.

A. Put parentheses around each main clause. Underline the subject once and the verb twice in each clause.

1. (You can meet us there), or (we will pick you up).

2. My friend was nervous, but I was not.

3. Gary will win, or I will eat my hat.

4. Jane mowed the lawn, and I watered it.

5. They vacationed in the mountains, and we went to the desert.

6. The drain was clogged, but Sam fixed it.

B. Here are some compound sentences and some simple sentences. Put *S* before each simple sentence. (As you know, in a simple sentence, the subject or the verb may be compound.)

Put *CD* before each compound sentence. (Remember: a compound sentence has two main clauses. Each clause has both a subject and a verb.)

_____ 1. Larry and Jeff were squad captains.

_____ 2. She cleaned and polished her car.

_____ 3. I had a cold, but now I am well.

_____ 4. Ron and Stan stopped and talked.

_____ 5. Ryan took his medicine, but he didn't like it.

_____ 6. Martha washed and ironed her dress.

_____ 7. She looked up the information, and I wrote it down.

_____ 8. The peaches weren't quite ripe, but they were still tasty.

_____ 9. Greg and I will paint the kitchen.

_____ 10. A test pilot's job is dangerous, and many men crack.

C. Use a compond sentence instead of two "baby" sentences that are closely related. In this exercise follow the model.

1. **I walk to school. Henry takes the bus.**
   I walk to school, but Henry takes the bus.
   _____

2. Canada is to the north. Mexico is to the south.
   _____

3. You must get a good night's sleep. You will feel tired tomorrow.
   _____

4. The lights went out. We couldn't see a thing.
   _____

5. Skiers like winter. I enjoy summer.
   _____

5. Complex Sentences

A *complex sentence* has one main clause and one dependent clause.

I missed school because I was sick.
   main clause   dependent clause

Plants are alive although they can't eat.
   main clause   dependent clause

A main clause, as you have seen, can stand by itself as a complete thought. This is not true of a dependent clause even though it has a subject and a verb.

A. Complete these sentences by writing a main clause or a dependent clause, as the case may be.

1. Jeff couldn't hear a word because _____.

2. If _____, should I give him the package?

3. When you want me, _____.

4. Although Barbara was angry, _____.

5. _____ since she moved to Boston.

B. Let's review the three kinds of sentences. In the blanks, write S if the sentence is simple, CD if it is compound, and CX if it is complex.

_____ 1. The country went wild when our astronauts landed on the moon.

_____ 2. Nancy and Ken left at the same time.

_____ 3. Before I could stop him, he jumped into the pool.

_____ 4. We were tired, but we won the contest.

_____ 5. Catherine sang and danced in the talent show.

_____ 6. Norma makes silk flowers, and Pam sells them.

_____ 7. The handsome deer ran proudly through the woods.

_____ 8. The sports dinner was postponed because the main speaker could not attend.

_____ 9. In the distance, we saw a beautiful lake.

_____ 10. I went to the store, but I forgot the milk.

C. In this exercise, combine two simple sentences into one complex sentence. Use the word in parentheses to form the dependent clause. Follow the two model sentences.

(UNLESS)   1. You can't fish in this lake. You must have a license.

<u>You can't fish in this lake unless you have a license.</u>

(WHILE)   2. It is raining. It is useless to wash the car.

<u>While it is raining, it is useless to wash the car.</u>

(AS)   3. The game will end soon. Let's start to leave.

_____

_____

(BECAUSE)   4. I can't buy a new tire. I don't have enough money.

_____

_____

(IF)   5. You are overweight. You should diet.

_____

_____

(WHEN)   6. The race will begin. The starter gives the signal.

_____

_____

(ALTHOUGH)   7. We scored six runs. We did not win the game.

_____

_____

A. Classify the following sentences according to their purpose. Write the correct letter in the blank space and supply the end punctuation.

S—statement   Q—question   R—request   E—exclamation

1. _____ Jill won the contest

2. _____ What a great prize this is

3. _____ How did you do it

4. _____ Hand me the scissors

5. _____ How beautiful the sunrise is

6. _____ Where are the directions

7. _____ They are in the glove compartment

8. _____ Hand them to me, please

9. _____ Does Jill have her driver's license yet

10. _____ He had a four-wheel drive pickup

B. Tell whether the italicized words are phrases or clauses. Write *P* or *C*.

_____ 1. The book fell *from the shelf.*

_____ 2. We must prepare for a useful job *because we want to earn a good living.*

_____ 3. *When the bell rang,* we were dismissed.

_____ 4. The note *on the bulletin board* is for you.

_____ 5. Come to my house *if you can.*

C. Label the following sentences as simple (*S*), compound (*CD*), or complex (*CX*).

_____ 1. When the dog barked, the stranger became frightened.

_____ 2. Chin made a mistake in spelling, and I corrected it.

_____ 3. My mother often misplaces her glasses.

_____ 4. If it is very windy, we will hold the party indoors.

_____ 5. Grandfather sat in the armchair, and soon he fell asleep.

D. In these compound sentences, underline the subject once and the verb twice in each clause.

1. The lawyer paused, and then he spoke.

2. The program was interesting, but it was a little too long.

3. You must help me, or I will never finish.

4. You should study hard, and you will make good grades.

5. The librarian dropped the book, and Clinton picked it up.

E. Label the main clause and the dependent clause in each complex sentence.

1. Let's have dessert after the table has been cleared.

2. If you come early, we can practice.

3. This is the spot where I found the pocketbook.

4. Because we had a flat tire, we were delayed.

5. The race stopped when a runner was injured.

F. You will be glad to hear that this is the final exercise. It is challenging, but it will prove your growth in English. If you do well, you will feel richly rewarded for your hard and careful work with _English, Plain and Simple_.

Below are groups of two or three weak sentences. Combine each group into one strong sentence.

1. **Plants need water. Plants need sunshine.**
   Plants need water and sunshine.
   _____

2. **It was 1981. The U.S. launched the first space shuttle.**
   In 1981, the U.S. launched the first space shuttle.
   _____

3. **A chicken has wings. It can't fly very well.**
   A chicken has wings, but it can't fly very well.
   _____

4. The sun rises in the east. The sun sets in the west.

_____

5. We have a car. It is a new car.

_____

6. He is tall. He is dark. He is handsome.

_____

7. A chair has legs. It can't walk.

_____

8. Rhode Island is a state. It is small.

_____

9. You snap the switch. The lights go on.

_____

10. Joe Louis was a championship boxer. Jack Dempsey was a championship boxer.

_____

11. Is the elevator going up? Is it going down?

_____

12. We buy eggs by the dozen. We buy milk by the quart. We buy meat by the pound.

_____

13. The American Revolution started. It happened at Lexington and Concord.

_____

14. You break the law. You will be in trouble.

_____

15. The American flag has stars. It has 50 stars.

_____

16. A frog has large eyes. A frog has a big mouth.

_____

17. Is the new baby a boy? Is it a girl?

_____

18. A radio won't work. A radio must have a battery.

_____

19. Theodore was a Roosevelt. Franklin D. was a Roosevelt. They were presidents.

_____

20. For daylight saving time, do we move our clocks ahead today? Do we move our clocks back?

_____

G. The "baby" sentences in these paragraphs are run together with no separation. Rewrite the paragraphs in "grown-up" English. You may add or drop words, as you like.

1. I checked my baggage I got on the plane it was my first flight I wasn't scared the view from my window was great I took several pictures time passed quickly.

_____

_____

_____

2. Tennis is a lot of fun I play it every chance I get it's easy to learn it's hard to play well you must be in good physical condition you will tire easily.

_____

_____

_____

_____